A Year in the Life

A Year in the Life

The Real Life Experiences of Your First Year Working as a School Building Administrator in a Public School

Dr. Jedrek Pillar

ROWMAN & LITTLEFIELD
Lanham • Boulder • New York • London

Published by Rowman & Littlefield
A wholly owned subsidiary of
The Rowman & Littlefield Publishing Group, Inc.
4501 Forbes Boulevard, Suite 200, Lanham, Maryland 20706
www.rowman.com

Unit A, Whitacre Mews, 26-34 Stannary Street, London SE11 4AB

Copyright © 2016 by Dr. Jedrek Pillar

All rights reserved. No part of this book may be reproduced in any form or by any electronic or mechanical means, including information storage and retrieval systems, without written permission from the publisher, except by a reviewer who may quote passages in a review.

British Library Cataloguing in Publication Information Available

Library of Congress Cataloging-in-Publication Data Available

ISBN 978-1-4758-2332-5 (hardcover)
ISBN 978-1-4758-2334-9 (e-book)

∞™ The paper used in this publication meets the minimum requirements of American National Standard for Information Sciences—Permanence of Paper for Printed Library Materials, ANSI/NISO Z39.48-1992.

Printed in the United States of America

This book is dedicated to my three girls:

*Lola,
Ana boo-boo,
and
Bennie boo-boo*

*Thank you for making every day fun, rewarding,
and a dream come true!*

I love you with all my heart!!!

Contents

Preface		ix
Introduction		xi
1	Here You Go	1
2	You Can't Make This Stuff Up	2
3	A Day in the Life of a School Administrator—Part I	7
4	A Day in the Life of a School Administrator—Part II	10
5	A Day in the Life of a School Administrator—Part III	16
6	A Day in the Life of a School Administrator—Part IV	20
7	A Day in the Life of a School Administrator—Part V	22
8	No Meds	26
9	You Can't Judge a Book by Its Cover	29
10	Keep Your Hands to Yourself	34
11	You Just Don't Understand	38
12	Let's Get Ready to Rumble	42
13	The Benefits of Being the Bad Cop	45
14	The Honeymoon Is Over	48
15	It's Not My Problem	51

16	Role Models	53
17	Those Who Can't Do, Teach	56
18	The Apple Doesn't Fall Far	58
19	The Art of Discipline	63
20	Comic Relief	67
21	Real Life	71
22	Priorities	74
23	A Visit from a Furry Friend	78
24	March Madness	81
25	When Push Comes to Shove	85
26	Not My Child	88
27	Things Are Not Always as They Appear	90
28	The Final Push	94
29	Food Fight	97
30	Help Who You Can	102
31	School's Out for Summer	104

Preface

Before I began working as a school building administrator, I felt as though I was well prepared for my new position. Since I had worked in the same building as a teacher, and I knew the faculty, staff, and many of the students, I believed I would hit the ground running. In my first days on the job, however, I was like a deer caught in headlights—wide-eyed and not certain what my next move should be. It did not take long for me to realize just how little I really knew coming into my new role.

Following my first week in my new position, my wife and I went out to dinner that Friday evening. Sitting at our table, she asked me how my day went. I answered her saying that the school day flew by, and proceeded to tell her about a parent meeting I had earlier that day. I shared how I had to explain to a student's mother why her daughter was sent to my office this early in the school year.

I continued to explain to this mother how her daughter was involved in a verbal altercation with another student. I told mom that earlier today her daughter had words with this other student and she threatened to scratch her eyes out in the girls' bathroom. Mom then expressed that she was so sick of her kids that she wanted Child Protective Services to take them away from her.

I was speechless. I had no idea how to respond.

My wife, who is not in education, was hanging onto my every word. She said she would have no idea of how to respond to this type of situation. I said neither did I.

I realized then that most people outside of education have no idea as to what goes on behind the scenes in public schools. I knew I certainly did not, and I was a teacher in the same building.

As the weeks and months passed by, I kept finding myself responsible for handling a wide range of student, parent, and teacher issues—all of which I had no prior experience dealing with. After much reflection on my experiences and how unprepared I felt I was for handling these situations, I believed that I would have benefited from a resource that could have given me a heads-up and better prepared me for what I could expect in my administrative position.

It was then that I decided to write a book about my first-year administrative experiences, and the lessons I learned along the way, as it could help aspiring administrators prepare for the responsibilities of their new positions. I knew that such a book would be beneficial for new administrators who, like me, have no idea what to expect in their first years as a dean, assistant principal, or principal of a public school building.

This book is as a valuable resource for aspiring school administrators, as it contains engaging, real-life stories that present a variety of challenging situations they can expect to encounter on the job. Following each story are helpful strategies and recommendations future and current administrators can reference when they find themselves as the lone person responsible for addressing these unpredictable, complex, and troubling issues.

This book is also an important resource for candidates preparing for interviews for administrative positions. Having the right answers for the "how to deal with difficult situations" questions, which this book provides, can go a long way toward separating you from your competition.

Overall, this book will give you a greater understanding of how to address and respond to critical situations, and help you feel more prepared as a school building administrator in addressing these serious issues when they come knocking on your door—which they undoubtedly will.

Introduction

This book takes you, the new building administrator, on an eye-opening journey through your first year on the job where you are working in a school building that is longing to regain order following the chaos that existed under the previous administrator's watch. The faculty and staff, whom you have worked alongside as a teacher for the past several years, are counting on you to get things back on track.

You begin your new position in September, the first month of the school year, and before you reach summer vacation in June, you will be charged with handling a wild series of unpredictable and unexpected situations along the way. It does not take long for you to realize that you have a lot to learn and that it is your responsibility to handle every troubling, shocking, heart-wrenching, and life-altering student issue that is brought to your attention.

As the year plays out and you race to follow up on every situation that comes your way, you learn a lot of valuable lessons and develop a greater understanding of what life is like as a building administrator in a public school. But, your journey only begins once the students return to school after summer vacation.

August is winding down and September is right around the corner. Your first year as a school building administrator is about to begin, so buckle up. You are in for a bumpy ride.

Chapter One

Here You Go

You are a first-year administrator in the same school in which you have been serving as a teacher for the last several years. The individual who held your current administrative position last year was let go for her poor job performance. With her at the helm, the building was in a terrible state. The saying "The inmates are running the asylum" was a fair assessment given the condition of your building under her reign.

The faculty's displeasure with both the job she did and the current culture of your building is at an all-time high. The entire faculty and staff have high expectations for you to come in and "right the ship" in your first year.

You work in a public middle school in Chicago, Illinois, that is located in a socioeconomically diverse suburb. The surrounding community of your school district has a variety of issues to deal with including poverty, violence, drugs, and gangs—and you have elements of these community conditions which seep into your building.

Your school building houses two grades, seventh and eighth, and there are close to 500 students per grade. This means there are almost 1,000 students, but only one you. The stories and events that follow can relate to all levels of public education (elementary, middle, and high schools) as well as schools located in more affluent or more struggling communities.

So, whether you are now, or are going to be, a principal, an assistant principal, or a dean, turn the page and see what you are about to get into. You may not believe what you are about to read, but try to remember, you can't make this stuff up!

Chapter Two

You Can't Make This Stuff Up

It is an average day in September, the first month of the school year, and you have a lot of work to do and not enough time to do it in. You are sitting at your desk, going through a dozen discipline referrals from the day before, when an eighth grade Spanish teacher, Ms. Gonzalez, comes into your office. You can see that she is visibly distraught and almost immediately she begins to cry. You ask her what is wrong and she proceeds to tell you about one of her students, Wade, who was just masturbating in her class.

Ms. Gonzalez describes the situation as best she can. "There was a glazed look in his eyes," she says nervously. She shifts her gaze between the floor and your eyes, opting only to look at you when not speaking. Her uncomfortable demeanor makes you feel sorry for her. There aren't many ways to comfortably describe a student masturbating in class, yet here she is, attempting the nearly impossible task of talking around the issue with euphemisms.

"The look in his eyes was like . . . like the lights were on, but nobody was home," she struggles to explain through a thick accent. She continues, "He was breathing heavily and then I heard him groaning. And he was rubbing his . . . his private area over his pants. He was sitting in the front of the classroom, and a little later, I saw a wet spot on his jeans." Ms. Gonzalez is clearly quite disturbed by this situation.

Once you finish gathering the particulars of the situation from Ms. Gonzalez, you decide to go to the principal to report this because, after all, this is your first month on the job.

You knock on her open office door, ask for permission to enter, and close the door behind you. As you sit down, she looks at you inquisitively from across her desk. You take a direct approach and say, "A student was masturbating in Spanish class this morning!"

She buries her head in her hands and tells you, "Get the hell out of here!" She does not mean for you to leave her office, literally, though. "You can't make this stuff up," she continues, shaking her head in disbelief. "Go ahead. Tell me what happened," she directs.

Following her prompt, you proceed to explain the situation as described to you by Ms. Gonzalez, making sure to include the specific details. Once you finish relaying the story, the principal picks up her phone and calls the school psychologist because, as she puts it, "This appears to be primarily an emotional issue."

The school psychologist speaks with Wade for about twenty minutes and afterward, you and he debrief. The school psychologist explains that Wade comes from a complex home situation, that he was adopted and his adoptive mother, a single parent, has recently been diagnosed with breast cancer.

When you hear this, your heart goes out to him. Not only did the only person who loved and cared for him receive a cancer diagnosis, you also know that quite often adopted children revisit their adoption during adolescence. They ask themselves, "Why? Why did my biological mother and father put me up for adoption?" You empathize with how hard it must be to be an eighth grade student with such heavy issues on your mind.

Unfortunately, following his conversation with Wade, the school psychologist shares with you that Wade was not the only in-school masturbator in the building. Apparently, last year Wade and one of his buddies started a contest where they competed to see who could "whack-off" the most number of times in school.

Now you understand that this morning's situation was actually part of a *competition* and you realize that you need to speak with Wade to get some clarification on this.

When you follow up with Wade regarding this new development, he refuses to divulge any additional information about who the other student is, when they began *competing*, or which other classes they masturbate in. Wade offers very few additional details about the contest, and given what the school psychologist had just told you about his family history and home life, you opt not to interrogate him.

You then reconnect with the principal to brief her on these latest developments. After listening to this new information on "the contest," she decides that this incident is no longer just an emotional issue but a discipline issue as well.

The school psychologist told you that he had already contacted Wade's mother to inform her of Wade's actions in Spanish class, but he said he made no mention of "the contest" during that conversation. You now have to call Wade's mom back to explain that a masturbation competition was taking place between her son and another student, and to inform her that Wade would receive one day of suspension (as per the principal's decision) as a consequence for participating.

An administrator for only ten school days, you are about to make your first phone call home regarding a student suspension. You have made plenty of phone calls home as a teacher, but those were about trivial classroom issues, such as disrupting class, failing exams, or not completing homework. You are in for a whole new type of parental contact.

When you call Wade's mother, she answers the phone and you can hear that she is still upset about the situation since she spoke with the school psychologist just a short while before your call. You identify yourself, but before you can get to the reason for your call, she questions you about the number of staff members who are aware of this incident.

"How many teachers are aware of this?" she asks desperately.

Caught off guard, you think quickly and answer, "I spoke with three educators about the incident. The classroom teacher who witnessed the incident, the principal, and the school psychologist."

In reality, you know an incident like this will spread like wildfire and that every staff member in the building will hear some version of this story by lunch time. You are not lying to Wade's mother, though, since at that point the truth was that you had only spoken with three of your colleagues about this situation.

Later that day, however, you learn that highly exaggerated versions of this incident are being widely discussed by faculty members via the "telephone" game. It won't be long before a number of them approach you with inquiries about the matter, and share what they have heard from the rumor mill. Before you are finished handling this issue, most of the teachers in the building will have heard of this story—except they will hear a morphed version of this situation where Wade stood up in front of the class, dropped his pants to masturbate, and yelled at Ms. Gonzalez until he ejaculated.

While your relationship with the faculty is in good standing at this point in the school year, your professional obligation to this student and his mother charge you to keep this information confidential. You make sure not to discuss the details of this situation when approached by teachers, but you do decide that you will inform them when something that they share with you about this situation is inaccurate.

Back to your phone call with mom: Even after you tell her that four educators, including yourself, are aware of what happened, she is still extremely distraught. Four is too high of a number for her comfort. Mom knows that everyone talks and probably figured that four would soon be eight, eight would become sixteen, sixteen would become thirty-two, and so on. You attempt to continue your conversation to get to the point of why you are calling.

You explain what you learned about the competition and say to mom, "I regret to inform you that, because it turns out that today's incident involving Wade was part of a contest between himself and another student, Wade will have a one-day suspension tomorrow."

Wade's mother does not respond to that piece of information well. "What? Well, my son won't even be in school tomorrow!" she says. "He'll be meeting with a doctor or a psychologist."

"Okay," you respond and, trying to make sure mom understands that there will be a consequence, you continue, "Just so you are aware, if your son is absent tomorrow, then he will serve one day of suspension the following school day."

After a moment of silence, she asks you, "Is that a threat?"

You attempt to make amends throughout the rest of this conversation, but to no avail. Wade's mother is too angry with you, and upset about the whole situation, to be talked down. She decides to come up to the school to meet with the building principal regarding the day of suspension and to complain about you.

Instead of making mom feel that the school was on her side and most concerned for her son's well-being, you helped to create an adversarial dynamic between her and you. While you were trying to make sure you followed up on the principal's orders in your telephone conversation with Wade's mother, you instead came across as though you were only concerned with suspending her son.

This is a tough phone call to make, especially for a new, first-year administrator. Not to worry, though, because handling a difficult situation such as this can be challenging for even the most veteran administrators.

As you reflect on this situation, it registers with you that you never even spoke with Wade about this allegation before you went to the principal. You realize that the prudent thing to do would have been to fully investigate the matter first, speaking with all parties involved, and then go to the principal with all of the comprehensive information. Things likely would have played out differently (much smoother) if you had done this.

You also realize how important it is to get on the same page with your colleagues and that it is probably best to make one phone call, along with the school psychologist, after all of the facts have been received and reviewed. This way, you are delivering these two messages in one conversation and you avoid the unnecessary "callback." You can deliver the information about the suspension first (to get the bad news out of the way). Then, the school psychologist can enter the conversation from an emotional and therapeutic standpoint and provide recommendations for outside resources and treatment.

Also, inviting Wade's mother into the school to discuss this situation in person can be an effective and personable way to communicate sensitive news such as this. Meeting with Wade's mother face to face and empathizing with how she felt may likely be the best way to communicate given this difficult situation.

Either way you choose, over the phone or in person, the school will show how it needs to respond to discipline issues while at the same time demonstrating its support and care for the student and his family.

This masturbation incident was quite the initiation for you, but as you will see over the course of this book, it could actually be viewed as one of the more mild incidents you will have to deal with as a school building administrator.

Chapter Three

A Day in the Life of a School Administrator—Part I

Something isn't right today and as you drive to work, you can feel it. Something about this day feels different. Something feels off. And it doesn't take long after you arrive to work for the unnerving premonition to begin revealing itself.

You are not in your office for more than five minutes when a parent shows up, unannounced, concerned about her eighth grade daughter, Lucy. Lucy has an older sister, Sarah, who should be in tenth grade but is not currently attending the high school due to her extensive history of delinquency. Their mother, Dawn, is concerned about Lucy because of the vast amount of trouble Sarah has gotten herself into in the past. Dawn does not want Lucy to go down the same path Sarah did.

You invite Dawn into your office and ask her to have a seat. You close your office door, sit down behind your desk, and begin listening to Dawn's concerns. In vivid detail, you learn more about the troubled past of Lucy's rebellious older sister. From staying out until six in the morning to being taken out of their home by the police in handcuffs, Sarah's troubled and out-of-control demeanor outside of school becomes increasingly evident to you. By the time the bell rings to start first period, Dawn has already shared with you that Sarah is now in rehab for her cocaine addiction.

As you listen to her mother, you realize that you knew Sarah from your teaching days in this building. You remember Sarah as being one of the most "frequent flyers" to the discipline office when she was here, getting into a barrage of trouble. That was a few years ago. Sarah should now be in tenth grade, but unfortunately, or fortunately rather, she checked into rehab instead.

Dawn, unsure of the future, explains to you how she does not want the history and dismal experiences of her older daughter to have a negative effect on Lucy. Distraught and mildly hysterical, Dawn continues to give you examples of Sarah's wrongdoings in more detail than you care to hear. As she begins to cry, you quietly slide the box of tissues on your desk in her direction.

At this point in the school year, it has only been a month for you in this new position, but you have already learned to expect at least three people crying in your office per day—whether they are students, parents, teachers, or fellow administrators. You have come to understand rather quickly that tissues are important to have, and you have stockpiled them in your office since they go so quickly.

Midway through your conversation with the sobbing mother, you attempt to refocus her as she takes a tissue.

"What is it you would like me to do?" you ask her.

"When you're dealing with my younger daughter, I would just appreciate if you keep these stories in mind," Dawn replies. "She's been exposed to a lot."

Now you see her point. She has made things clear and you believe her to be a genuinely concerned and loving parent. But the tissue is barely dry before she begins to cry again. She takes another tissue.

This single mother sits with her head slightly bowed, ripping pieces of tissue on her lap and twirling the fragments between her fingers. Between quiet sobs, she lifts the tissue to dab her eyes, meeting your gaze every few seconds. Her eyes, you notice, seem to be the victims of many tears, and drooping cheekbones are the worn remainders of her once youthful face.

"A couple of months ago, Sarah tried to jump out of the passenger seat door while I was driving," she says softly. She pauses through her tears, glancing nervously around the room before she adds, "I wish she would have been killed that day."

You do your best to refrain from reacting or revealing signs of emotion on your face, but inwardly, you are blown away. You half wonder if you heard her incorrectly. But any doubts you have are quickly eliminated as she continues to repeat herself, her words gaining more confidence with each syllable.

"I wish she would have been run over," she says. "I wish she would've been killed. That way . . ."

Your heart begins to break. "How can a parent say this about her child?" you wonder. "If she feels comfortable enough to say this to someone she just met less than an hour ago, what on earth does she say to her friends? What does she say at home?"

You are not going to begin to concede that you have a good understanding of how frustrating her family situation might be, but you don't need to know more about her home life to see that there is something terribly wrong here.

You imagine that there are times when the students in your building drive their parents crazy, literally. The late-night news reports stories of parents who murder their entire families and then commit suicide, but this up-close and personal account caught you blindsided.

This meeting with Dawn shed a lot of light on the dysfunction that must exist in their house, and on some possibilities as to why Sarah was so troubled. You let Dawn know that you will keep an eye on Lucy, and that you will call her immediately if you have any concerns. You then shake hands and say, "Goodbye," as Dawn leaves your office.

There is no easy way to address the situation. Of course, you will make sure to keep an eye and ear out for Lucy and report any concerns you have to Dawn, but contacting CPS (Child Protective Services) also crosses your mind. In response to the outrageous statements this mother has made, you are not sure if reporting this issue to CPS is the right move.

Your best bet, especially being a new administrator with only one month of the school year under your belt, is to go and share this information with the building principal. Communicating the conversation you had with this parent, and your question about contacting CPS, with other administrators who have more work experience is a smart move given all the circumstances here.

You look at the clock and it is now 9:00 a.m. First period still has about five minutes left in it, but you already feel that you have completed a full day's work, as this conversation with Dawn has taken a lot out of you. That does not matter, though, because this day is not about to slow down for you.

Chapter Four

A Day in the Life of a School Administrator—Part II

The next issue brought to your attention involves a stolen cell phone, but your investigation will surface a situation much more important than missing electronic equipment. You already felt your heart break one time today, so you don't think it's possible that you can feel any worse. But for the second time in this early morning, your assumptions will be proved wrong.

It is now ten minutes after 9:00 a.m. and the second unexpected parental visit this morning comes rushing into your office.

"My daughter's cell phone was just stolen!" Roger, the parent, says abruptly. "And I have a good idea who took it." Roger and his daughter, Megan, come into your office to report that they believe a student named James took the phone out of her pocketbook in their technology class.

You quietly reserve judgment as you listen to Roger because you know there are always two sides to every story. While Roger could have legitimate reasons behind his accusations, Megan, in reality, could have lost her cell phone outside of school and just been afraid to admit that to her father.

Students lying to their parents, saying that something was stolen in school when it wasn't, is another occurrence you have gotten used to rather quickly—even this early in the school year. You have found that some kids find it easier to lie to their parents and tell them something was stolen in school because it focuses their parents' attention on what the school did wrong, rather than on their own child. Therefore, in this case, you understand it is important that you do not assume James is guilty without fully investigating this situation first.

You begin looking into this allegation by calling for James and having him sent to your office. James is a short, chubby seventh grader with big eyes and an even bigger smile. He is a very likable kid who comes from a poverty-stricken, single parent home and you find yourself secretly hoping that he is innocent. Still, you know you have to question him about Megan's missing cell phone.

When it comes to investigating potential thefts, you often take an approach that you learned from some of the veteran administrators you have worked with in the past and you decide to employ this strategy in this situation. You never want students to have their guards up when you are questioning them about a discipline issue. If the student in question stole something and senses that you are questioning him about the missing property, you know that you'll have a tough time getting the truth out of him.

In such investigations, you start by asking the student a couple of questions such as "How was your weekend?" or "Have you seen any good movies lately?" The students usually respond immediately because there is no need for them to think of a lie to those questions. You then ask a third question related to the stolen property. If the student is innocent, then they will answer the third question without hesitation because they don't have anything to hide. If the student is guilty, though, there will be a pause before they answer the third question because they are now thinking before they respond. Since you feel a responsibility to do what you can to get Megan's property back, this is the approach you decide to take with James as you both sit in your office.

"So what's your favorite class?" you ask.

He smiles and quickly answers, "Math."

"Who do you have for math?" you reply. He answers with the name of his teacher and you almost dread proceeding. After starting with two icebreaker questions, you reluctantly move on to your real question.

"Do you have a cell phone that doesn't belong to you?" you ask. You see his facial expression immediately change from relaxed to concerned. He does not answer initially. Rather, he reaches into his pocket, pulls out the cell phone in question, and hands it to you, saying, "I was going to give it to you."

You have conducted investigations similar to this one already this school year, so you now know that it is very unlikely that James innocently found this phone. If he did find the phone and had every intention of turning it in, why did he wait until he was called down to your office and questioned to give it to you? You know that a suspension is imminent.

You then ask James how he came into possession of the cell phone, still hoping for the highly unlikely scenario that he did not steal it from Megan's pocketbook.

James explains that he found the phone on the hallway floor near his locker. You know immediately that he is lying because his whole affect is different than it was when you were asking him about his math class. He is now fumbling over his words and his perpetual bouncing knee is a dead giveaway that he is anxious about telling the truth. You know where this is going.

At this point, you ask James if what he has told you is the truth and he responds that it is. You tell him that you are going to check the video footage of the hallway cameras to confirm his story. You leave him in your office for a couple of minutes while you go and "check the cameras."

There are cameras all over the building, but they are in fixed positions and do not capture every inch of the hallways. While you know that where James claims he found the phone is out of the closest camera's range, you also know that James is lying to you. So, without actually checking the videotape, you decide to throw a bluff out there.

After killing two minutes of time chatting with a teacher you happened to run into in the hallway, you return to your office, sit down, look at him, and say, "You know what I am going to say, don't you?" If there is a chance that he is telling you the truth, he will call your bluff and stick to his story.

Instead, James begins crying and you respond by sliding the tissue box in his direction. After taking several tissues, James changes his story, telling you, "I found the phone in the boy's locker room." You realize he probably said this because he knows for certain there are no cameras in the locker rooms.

"James, I know that is not the truth either," you reply with your eyes looking into his, pleading with him to stop this charade.

If he already told you one lie, you have little to no reason to believe that his second story is the truth, especially since it does not coincide with the rest of the details of this situation. Also, you had already made a point to review James's class schedule and noticed that he did not have physical education this morning. Therefore, he had no reason to be in the boys' locker room.

After a minute of him squirming, he changes his story once again and says, "I found it in technology class." You answer to him, "Now we are getting a little closer to the truth."

After a few more minutes of your questioning James, he finally admits to taking the phone out of Megan's pocketbook and apologizes.

You make a point to approach these types of investigations with your chief concern being to get the victim's property back. However, even when the victims do get their property back, you understand that there still needs to be consequences for the guilty party—even if they eventually admit to their mistakes and apologize. If someone robs a bank, gets caught, returns the money, and apologizes, they are still going to prison. You feel like you do not want to punish James, but now it is clear to you that he did steal another student's property and he needs to be held accountable for it.

Once James comes clean, he begins sobbing uncontrollably—and he is not a conniving student who can pull the wool over your eyes with crocodile tears. You see that he is legitimately scared to death about what is going to happen to him when his mother finds out what he did.

This harmless, overweight, eleven-year-old boy is crying so uncontrollably hard that he can barely breathe, much less speak. There are so many tears coming out of James's eyes that his entire face is soaked and you actually find yourself concerned that he may become dehydrated.

James is so worried about what will happen when you tell his mother what he did that he begs you, "Please don't tell my mom! Please don't tell my mom!"

"I have to, James," you answer, barely holding back some tears yourself. Again he pleads, "Please, please don't tell my mom!" Trying your best to remain stoic, you ask, "Why don't you want me to tell your mom?"

He sobs through his reply, "Because if you tell my mom . . . then I . . . then I will have to go live with my dad. My mom said that the next time I . . . I get in trouble, I would have to go live with my dad. I don't want . . . to live with . . . my dad. Please! I don't want to live with my dad!"

"Why don't you want to go live with your dad?" you ask, trying hard to keep your voice from cracking.

"I don't want to live . . . with my dad," he repeats, growing more emotional with each passing second, "I'm not allowed to tell you why. My mom told me that I can't say why. Please, don't tell my mom! I don't want to go live with my dad!"

Your heart breaks for the second time this morning. In order to do your job and enforce your building's Code of Conduct for student behavior, are you going to have to completely turn James's entire life upside down and send him to live in a less desirable situation than he is already in? You are becoming more and more conflicted about this situation.

Sitting across from James you think to yourself, "What am I doing here? How am I helping students in this situation? Am I doing any good at all?"

You got into this field because you care about kids. You never wanted students to feel this much fear for their well-being. To be this young and scared of living with your father is just sad. You think to yourself, "What am I going to do here?"

Because James is so emotional about his family situation, you refer him to the school social worker. After speaking with James, the social worker comes back and reports to you that he feels that James's father is not physically abusive toward his son. You hope that is the truth.

You then contact James's mother and ask her to come up to school so you can explain this situation to her in person.

After meeting with James and his mother, explaining the mistake James made, how remorseful and apologetic he was in your conversation with him, the unavoidable suspension he will have to serve, and his fears about living with his father, mom rubs James's head and reassures him that he is not going to live with his dad. James, finally, is calm and at peace.

Seeing James's mother console him and reassure him that everything will be alright is a much needed "pick-me-up" for you. At the end of this situation, the most important items were taken care of: The matter with James's family was smoothed over and Megan got her phone back.

While you may question or reconsider your approach to this investigation in terms of ethics in your questioning and interviewing of James, remember that your paramount concern initially was to get Megan's property back, which you successfully did. Then, when you learned of James's concerns about going to live with his father, that became your top priority and you helped to alleviate James's concerns in your conversation with him and his mother, so you should feel good about that. In the end, you are entitled to a well-deserved pat on the back for how you handled this situation. You got to the bottom of the missing cell phone situation and you smoothed things over with James and his mother in the process.

It is now only the middle of second period and there are another six and a half periods left to go in this eight-period school day.

You recall what you were thinking while driving to the building not more than two hours ago. How and why did you sense this on your way to work this morning? Before you can attempt to answer your own questions, though, the door to your office opens again and in walks a sexual harassment issue.

Chapter Five

A Day in the Life of a School Administrator—Part III

You feel as though the first couple of periods lasted an eternity, and just as you are coming to grips with all that has happened already this morning, you receive information about a male student, Nate, sexually harassing a female student, Sharon, in their music class.

"What the hell?" you think to yourself. "It's 9:15 a.m. on a Monday morning. How can all of this be happening already?"

Now you understand why other administrators asked you when you were still in college, "Are you sure you want to go into administration?" Your answer to them was always something like, "Yes. I would like to serve students and a school district on a greater scale."

On this particular day, however, you are not so sure that you do.

Sharon enters your office, unannounced and without knocking, sits down across from your desk, and describes the uncomfortable and creepy look in Nate's eyes as he stared at her in their music class. Sharon tells you how Nate moved his seat next to hers and how he refused to stop rubbing her knee under her desk, even after she told him "Stop!" five times. She continues to share how she then slapped him in the face to put a halt to his aggressions, how Nate pushed her in retaliation, and how she then countered his push with a punch to his groin.

As Sharon explains what has just happened, you can't help but wonder where the teacher was during all of this commotion. When you ask the music teacher a short time later to find out, she asserts that she did not witness anything.

"Not the touching, the slap, the push, or the punch?" you ask her.

"No, I didn't see anything," she answers.

"Nothing? Nothing at all?" you respond.

"No, I didn't see anything," she repeats.

You refrain from expressing your disdain for her lack of awareness because it will not make a difference given the current situation. Wagging your finger at this teacher would be unproductive and you know this. She did not witness the incident, and your voicing your disappointment with her will not change what has happened in her class.

After Sharon finishes telling you what transpired between her and Nate, you send her to the guidance office and have her speak with her counselor. You then pull Nate from class and begin questioning him about this situation. Nate denies any part he had in this, which does not surprise you.

Veteran school building administrators know, but will never admit, that the best defense mechanism for students who are guilty is to deny, deny, deny. It's hard to hold students accountable for their indiscretions without solid evidence of their wrongdoings or a confession from them.

You have seen law enforcement television programs where detectives interrogate suspects to draw information from them or get them to confess: The small gray room with the table in the middle of the floor, the *perp* on one side of the table and the investigators on the other.

Investigating a complaint or allegation as a school building administrator can be a lot like that, albeit on a much smaller scale.

After fifteen minutes of speaking with Nate, questioning him and shooting holes in his stories, he finally admits to you his part in this situation and confirms the story Sharon had told you. You take your notes on his admission to the building principal and share this information with her, and she calls Nate into her office, where she expresses her disgust with his behavior.

With you sitting quietly on the couch in her office and Nate standing at attention in front of her desk, she asks him in a stern voice, "How would you feel if a man treated your mother or sister like this? Wouldn't you be upset if someone tried to hurt her or make her do something she didn't want to do?" She goes on to let him know how upset she is, detailing the qualities of a good man before giving him a multi-day out-of-school suspension.

The following week, after Nate served his suspension, he returns to his music class and immediately begins staring Sharon down to intimidate her. He feels that she had gotten him into trouble and he is very angry about that. Not more than two minutes later, Sharon is back in your office, again unannounced, and more shaken up than the first time.

Sharon again explains what has happened and you follow the same process you did the first time around: You listen to her, send her to her guidance counselor, call Nate into your office, question him, eventually get his admission, and then walk him back to the principal's office.

In a similar but more intense fashion as before, the principal lectures Nate in a disapproving tone. This conversation lasts longer, each word more unrelenting than the last, and her tone is harsher than the previous time Nate was in her office. Nate would be suspended out of school once again.

As a result of the adamant request of Sharon's mother, who is understandably furious about this situation, the principal decides to switch Sharon's schedule so she will no longer share her music class with Nate.

As will likely be the case in your school, class change requests from students and parents will very rarely be honored. If they are, such requests will be never ending because people in the community talk and if you do for one, you have to do for all. However, given the circumstances of Sharon and Nate's history in this case, switching Sharon's schedule is the right thing to do for her safety and well-being.

Even though there is a zero tolerance policy for hitting another student in school, you quietly applaud Sharon for the way she handled this situation. You are proud of her and feel that it was great that she stood up for herself and refused to be treated like an object by Nate. While she did take matters into her own hands initially, at the end of the day she asserted herself, reported what had happened to building administration, and effectively put an end to this harassment.

You also handled the situation appropriately, but there is always room for improvement. In terms of the music teacher who stated that she did not witness the altercation between Sharon and Nate, you can make strong recommendations for that teacher to improve her "with-it-ness" in her classroom going forward. After you explained the sexual harassment issue that occurred under her watch, you should have stressed the importance of her being more aware of students' behaviors in her classroom and instructed her to keep a close eye on the interactions between Nate and Sharon going forward.

Hindsight is 20/20, but had you done this after the first incident (because clearly you cannot rely on this teacher to be self-reflective and raise her awareness in her classroom on her own), the follow-up "stare down" incident may never have occurred. The bottom line is, when you are dealing with teachers like this, do not assume they will learn from their mistakes on their own. You will need to give them clear feedback and recommendations on how to improve their practice when situations such as these arise.

The end of second period is now approaching. After returning from the principal's office you are sitting at your desk, completing the paperwork for Nate's first suspension, when you hear the discipline office door quickly opening. Someone, who is apparently in a hurry, is coming to see you. You know this can't be good.

Chapter Six

A Day in the Life of a School Administrator—Part IV

The bell to end second period sounds, and you hear your office door open. You are getting used to the reality that whenever you hear the sound of your office door opening, anyone and anything could be coming your way. You look up and see a student's mother entering. She looks angry. She's coming to speak with you about a phone call you made to her the previous week regarding her son, Keith. In that phone call, you had informed her of the buzz going around the school that Keith is in a gang.

Like some parents who receive unwelcomed information about their child, she takes a defensive stance with you. She is a single mother and, with no one else to let loose on, you as the messenger become her outlet. While in your office, she defends her child's innocence and berates you as though you made up this accusation on your own. In reality, though, you know it is Keith himself who has been spreading the rumor that he is in a gang.

Personally, you don't believe that Keith is in a gang because you know him well enough to know that he oftentimes says things to get the attention of others. Your gut tells you that he most likely wanted to appear as a tough guy in his classmates' eyes. Keith is a low-functioning, self-contained student, which means that he is in one classroom throughout the school day with four other special-needs students and two teachers. Keith has a very low IQ and you suppose he hardly understands the severity of what he has been saying, in terms of the potential ramifications both inside and outside of school. Even though you seriously doubt that Keith is in a gang, you know it is your responsibility to take precautionary action and inform the parent of what you are hearing.

Mom vehemently argues with you that her son is not in a gang and she blames you for wrongfully labeling him as a thug gang-banger. You initially try to tell her that you are simply sharing information that her son is telling other students in the building, and that he is not in any serious trouble in school at this time, but you cannot get a word in edgewise. She is yelling over you every time you try to explain this. You decide to stop talking and just listen while you let Keith's mother vent.

After almost twenty minutes of letting her blow off steam, you see an opening and try again to reiterate your points to her. This time she starts to listen. She is finally paying attention to you and she begins to understand that you are sharing important information that you know that she, as a concerned parent, would want to be made aware of so she can discuss this situation with her son. In the end your conversation with Keith's mother concludes nicely, and she thanks you for your efforts and concern, but it was a bumpy road getting here.

As long as you are a school building administrator, you will have to deal with irate and irrational parents. It's part of the job, so you might as well get used to it. The more angry parents you speak with, the better you will become at handling these difficult conversations. In this situation, you did a nice job because you eventually got Keith's mother to listen to reason and hear what you were trying to tell her.

Next time, however, you will choose to sit back and listen to these incensed parents right from the beginning because you now know that there is no sense in talking if they are not ready to listen to what you have to say. Letting these parents express their concerns, frustrations, or fears first, so they get them off of their chest, will enable them to listen to you once you finally get the opportunity to speak.

This will not work with every upset parent that seeks you out, mind you, because some moms and dads remain angry even after they have gone off yelling at you for a half an hour. But most parents are reasonable and just concerned with their child's well-being, so this "wait-to-speak" approach will work more often than not.

It is now almost the end of third period and you finally get a moment of peace. You go to the bathroom to splash some cold water on your face. "What else could happen today?" you think to yourself. Standing over the sink, you look at your reflection in the mirror and say, "There is going to be a fight today." You are not sure why you just said this out loud since you are the only one in the bathroom, but the way this day has started has you talking to yourself about what will follow.

Chapter Seven

A Day in the Life of a School Administrator—Part V

Shortly after fourth period begins, you are informed there was a fight in the cafeteria. It turns out that you are right about your prediction. Well, sort of.

You learn that a couple of boys were fooling around, playing the game "two for flinching" during lunch, when things got out of hand. You have heard of this *game*, which basically works like this: If you make someone flinch by pretending to hit them, you say, "Two for flinching," and punch them twice in the arm.

Well, these two boys were playing "two for flinching," going back and forth, making each other flinch and punching each other in the arm. That is, until one boy punched the other a little too hard. Then the fun and games stopped. The boys started punching each other harder and harder in the arms, disregarding the flinching component of the game. Then the boys' punches moved from each other's arms to each other's faces.

The cafeteria monitors broke up the fight and escorted both boys to your office. After speaking with the students involved, and confirming the information that had been shared with you, you have the school nurse look at them to make sure they do not require further medical attention. Both boys have some bruises, but they are otherwise fine. You then call both sets of parents, ask them to come up to the school to pick up their children, and inform them that their sons will be suspended out of school for the next three days.

You recall the brief moment of peace you had in the bathroom and realize you should have said, "There are going to be two fights today." Then your prediction would have been accurate because shortly after sixth period begins, two female students get into a fight in the hallway.

Reportedly, one girl *accidentally* bumped into the other, but the other girl did not believe that it was an accident so she *purposefully* pushed her back. Pushes turned to grabs, grabs turned to slaps, and slaps turned to punches and before you know it, you have yourself a second fight to handle today.

A couple of nearby teachers broke the two girls apart and escorted them down to your office. Going through the same steps you just followed with the boys, you gather their stories, have the school nurse look at them, notify their parents, have the parents come in to pick up their daughters from the building, and assign two three-day out-of-school suspensions.

By the time you sit with each of the parents to discuss the circumstances of what happened and their children's suspensions for fighting, it is eighth period and almost time for dismissal. You are exhausted and you desperately want this day to be over!

Not so fast.

In a sad state of irony, even after most of the students go home following dismissal, the day does not end for you. There is still after-school detention today and given the way the rest of this day has gone, it only figures that there would be something else you need to handle before your workday is over and you can go home.

You are now back in your office, checking your "in" pile, which you have not had one moment to look at yet today, when you receive a phone call from the main office informing you that you are needed to go to the detention room to remove two unruly students from detention.

You walk to the detention room and direct the two students to grab their things and come with you to the main office. While they do eventually pick up their belongings and comply with your directions, they do so at a snail's pace and have plenty to say to you while doing so.

They are completely incorrigible and continue to give you lip as the three of you walk from the detention room to the main office. When you attempt to reprimand them for their behaviors, they start feeding off of each other. As one of the students tells you off, saying, "You can't do anything about it!" the other one joins in, telling you, "You're a joke!"

You are now running on empty. After the day you just had, you are completely out of patience and growing more agitated by the minute.

The three of you enter the main office and you start making the parent phone calls. You get in touch with both sets of parents to inform them of their children's behaviors and of their resulting one-day suspensions for their gross insubordination.

As you are speaking with one of the parents on the phone, you notice out of the corner of your eye that the two students are writing something on pieces of paper.

You then realize what they are doing. The principal has a suggestion box located in the main office and students are encouraged to write down their recommendations on how they feel their school can be improved and deposit them in the suggestion box for the principal to read.

After you finish with both parent phone calls, you tell the students that they can now leave the building and that their parents expect them to walk directly home. The two students drop their pieces of paper in the suggestion box, walk out of the main office, and then out of the building.

After they leave you are still worked up, so you decide to open the suggestion box and read their *suggestions*.

Both suggestions colorfully suggest to "fire this new a**hole!" Of course, they go on to identify you as the "new a**hole" in their written suggestions.

Oddly enough, you feel better after reading them. To you, these suggestions, coming from these students, means that you are doing your job, which your predecessor failed miserably to do properly. After a grueling and exhausting day, you put the suggestions back in the principal's suggestions box, collect your things, and drive home from work calm, at peace, and with a smile on your face.

This was certainly an atypical day for you, but representative of the types of days you will encounter as a school building administrator just the same. You handled the student fights in a fine fashion and the only thing you feel a little regret over is your decision to check the principal's suggestion box at the end of the day. You feel this was morally wrong because these suggestions were really meant for the principal's eyes and not necessarily yours.

You are human, however, and at the end of this long day, you were completely out of patience. And don't forget, it was reading those students' recommendations that put you back at ease and in a calm and happy state of mind for your ride home.

Perhaps next time you will be more accustomed to handling the many tasks and responsibilities that will come your way on days like today, and therefore you will not take personally what the two students from the detention room said to you. That "thick skin" will come with time, so it is understandable that you could lose your patience after having a day like you just did, especially this early in your new position. But you handled and followed up on everything that came to your attention today and you should be proud of that.

While thinking about your drive to work this morning on your commute home, you still can't figure out why you had the feeling that something would be different today. No matter, though. The one thing you do know is that you are working very hard and your efforts are making a difference.

Chapter Eight

No Meds

There are some kids who get in trouble so frequently in school that it becomes clear to you and the rest of the faculty and staff that they just cannot control themselves. They don't realize that what they are doing is wrong and everyone seems to understand that it is not even their fault.

There is one particular student in your school, Sam, who is one of those kids. Sam has some pretty severe behavioral and social issues, and is frequently in your office as a result. He has an extensive history of grabbing and wrestling other students without provocation, and often these interactions result in physical altercations. Sam just doesn't get it. He can't get it.

You know Sam is not a rotten kid, though he is certainly troubled due to his undiagnosed case of ADHD (Attention Deficit Hyperactivity Disorder). ADHD is a common disorder in adolescents, and students with ADHD have difficulty staying focused and controlling their behavior. Everyone in your building who knows Sam knows he has ADHD.

One day, Sam was sent to your office for what he described as "doodling" on a classroom desk. However, as you learned from the classroom teacher, this is what actually happened:

Sam was holding a ballpoint pen upside down in his closed fist and driving the tip of the pen into the top of his desk. Oblivious to his teacher's directives for him to stop, he continued driving the tip of the pen into the desk for the better part of the period. Sam applied so much force that the ballpoint of the pen broke off and ink poured out all over the desk, the classroom floor, and on Sam himself. It made such a mess that ink stains remained on the desk, the floor, and Sam's hands for weeks.

Another time Sam was sent to your office, he told you that he "dropped" his pencil and that it *accidentally* poked one of his classmates in the leg. After doing some investigating, you learned what really happened:

Sam's pencil fell off of his desk and onto the floor during his music class. As Sam bent down from his chair to pick it up, the classmate sitting next to him tried to be a wise guy and gather the pencil with his foot so Sam could not get to it. Sam persisted in trying to pick up his pencil and when he ultimately got it out from under his classmate's sneaker, he squeezed the pencil in his hand and thrust the sharpened point directly into his classmate's thigh. The pencil point went through his classmate's jeans and snapped off, breaking his skin and remaining lodged in his leg. Sam used his pencil as a weapon and received a significant out-of-school suspension for this incident.

These were only two of the many instances where Sam was sent to your office for being unable to control himself in school. You genuinely feel bad for Sam because you know that there is no help for him in sight. Unfortunately, his father refuses to follow up on the school's strong and repeated recommendation that he seek outside treatment for Sam.

It takes you and your colleagues months of phone calls and parent conferences before Sam's father finally decides to follow the school's recommendations and take Sam to see a doctor. Once he finally did, though, Sam was quickly diagnosed as having ADHD and prescribed medication to help him focus and curb his impulsivity.

A few weeks after dad's follow-up, Sam comes to your office to report that another student, Marc, is teasing him by chanting his name over and over, "Sa-am! Sa-am!" Given Sam's significant behavioral history, you are astonished that he came to your office to report this.

Ordinarily, you would tell any other student with this sort of complaint to ignore Marc and not let it get to them. But in this instance, and possibly for the first time, Sam is the victim. He was doing his best to pay no attention to Marc and the mere fact that he had not yet resorted to violence is a big deal. You, therefore, take the opportunity to praise Sam for exercising his self-control and you encourage him to keep up the good work.

Sam is so taken aback by hearing something positive about his behavior that he does not know how to respond to you. He doesn't say anything back initially. Then, after almost a full minute of silence, he mutters, "Thanks."

On almost every other occasion when Sam was in your office, he was being reprimanded for his behavior. For just about any other student you would not make such a big deal about *not* turning to violence because that should be a given. But with Sam, you know it is important to commend him for taking this level-headed approach.

This was a big step in the right direction for Sam. He finally controlled himself and you know it is because he took his meds today.

Now, Sam is just one of the frequent flyers you have in your building. The rest of your high-profile students exhibit delinquent behaviors, but not necessarily because they are not properly medicated. If you want to get the names of *all* of the frequent flyer students in your building, in an effort to take some proactive measures to build positive relationships with them and curb their delinquency in school, then there are a number of steps you can take.

Speaking with your principal and fellow building administrators at the beginning of the school year and asking them if there are certain students they think you should be aware of is a good first step. Then, following up with these students' guidance counselors and other school support personnel to ask them if they have important information on these students they can share with you would be a good follow-up.

You can also choose to reach out to the parents of these students to make some positive contact with them early on in the school year. Inviting the parents and their child in for a meeting with you to discuss how you can best support them is a nice way to demonstrate your care for their child and open lines of communication with them that can last for the rest of the school year.

Beyond that, your interactions and conversations with these students will help you paint a pretty clear picture of what these students' needs are and what you can do to help them be successful in school.

Chapter Nine

You Can't Judge a Book by Its Cover

There's a lot of truth in the old adage "You can't judge a book by its cover," but that phrase means so much more to you now that you are a school building administrator.

You realize that the way a student appears, and the opinions others form about them, has very little to do with who they really are on the inside. Unfortunately, you also realize that in a school environment an individual's image is often created and shaped by the gossip of others.

As an administrator, you are privy to some of the most heinous gossip in your building and, possibly as a result, you have learned that you cannot judge someone based on the preconceived notions of others. It's embarrassing for educators to admit, but a student's reputation in school is determined not just by the gossip of their peers but from what faculty and staff members say about them as well.

Your building houses only seventh and eighth graders, and the sixth graders have their own building. Each year there is gossip among the teachers between the two buildings about the incoming sixth graders. Consequently, some kids who were problem students in sixth grade do not have a fair chance at the "clean slate" they were promised in middle school.

There is one former sixth grader in particular whose reputation preceded her first day as a seventh grader. From your days as a welcomed teacher in the faculty lounge, you recall hearing of a student named Abbey, and how she is *one bad seed*. Abbey did not know it, but she came into your building with the deck already stacked against her.

When you first met Abbey it was during the annual opening grade-level meeting, which your school holds with the entire incoming seventh grade class during the first week of the school year. In this meeting, you noticed a chubby, brown-haired girl with crooked teeth and glasses. She answered a question you posed to the students about the differences between the sixth grade building and the middle school. You were impressed with her answer, so after the meeting you went up to her and introduced yourself. You asked her what her name was and she answered, "Abbey."

You did a double take. This was the Abbey you had heard about in the faculty lounge. You made sure to stop your bias from showing on your face by smiling, greeting her warmly, and welcoming her to the building.

Right after meeting Abbey, you headed to your office, looked up her class schedule, and printed it out. You made a point to keep an eye out for her over the first couple of weeks of school, but as time would tell, Abbey never got into trouble. After all of the talk in the faculty lounge, you never heard any complaints from her teachers. Not one.

However, you also recall there was another student, Linda, sitting behind Abbey at the grade-level meeting who kept chatting with her friends during the presentation. With her blond hair, big blue eyes, and bright smile, Linda looked like an innocent little angel. For such a sweet-looking girl, Linda would turn out to be far more devious and underhanded than her *cover* would let on.

Over the course of Linda's seventh grade year, this little "angel" finds her way to the discipline office almost forty times. That is like being sent to your office every single week of the school year. "Funny," you think to yourself, "I never heard anything about Linda from the teachers in the faculty lounge."

One day, while dealing with the daily conundrums of the job, you receive a phone call from Ms. Walters, the mother of another student, regarding Linda's offhand behavior.

"I have an issue with the way one of the young girls in your school spoke to my daughter," she begins firmly. "At rehearsal for the music concert after school yesterday, Linda told my daughter, Molly, to go and shave her vagina!"

As you wait for Ms. Walters to proceed, an awkward pause hangs like dead air between the two of you. As the seconds pass, you realize that mom is not pausing to continue; she is waiting for your response. You become aware of this and try to pull together the right words.

"According to what you are telling me, this sounds like a serious situation, Ms. Walters." You continue, "Is this the first time Molly has mentioned this type of behavior from Linda?"

"As far as I know, it is the only instance involving my daughter. Is there something I don't know!?" she bites at you.

Ms. Walters is becoming more heated as your conversation goes on. Similar to your conversation with Keith's mom, when her son was spreading rumors around school that he is in a gang, Ms. Walters is speaking with you as though this is your fault, as if you are the one who instructed Linda to tell her daughter to shave her vagina, as if you knew about the situation beforehand and did nothing to stop it.

"No, ma'am," you try to empathize, "I just want to make sure I understand this entire situation so I can address this issue properly."

Ms. Walters and you speak for another couple of minutes and you learn that Molly is not the only victim of Linda's antics. Mom shares with you that Linda also told a boy to shave his vagina as well. You conclude your phone conversation by telling Ms. Walters that you will take this matter, and your investigation into it, seriously.

Right after you hang up the phone, you call Linda into your office to question her. As she sits across from your desk, you seriously doubt Linda would say such vulgar things to other students. Ms. Walters must have given you the wrong name. You get right to the point and ask Linda if she told two other students to shave their vaginas yesterday at rehearsal.

"I never said to shave your vagina," Linda attempts to innocently convince you.

"You didn't?" you respond. You find yourself believing her.

"No," she answers with a feeble smirk on her face. A long strand of blond hair hangs adorably in front of her left eye, swaying slightly whenever she moves her head. She is sitting up straight and has her hands folded politely on her crossed legs. When she speaks, she looks you straight in the eyes, each word more confident than the last.

"So what did you say, then?" you ask just as a follow-up.

"I said *faginas*," she replies, as if this clears up everything and this was all one big misunderstanding. She clarifies again, "I told them to go shave their *faginas*."

"*Faginas*?" you repeat. "What are *faginas*?"

"I don't know," she answers. "They're nothing. I just said it."

"Yeah right," you think to yourself. It is at this moment that you realize that you cannot believe another word that comes out of Linda's mouth.

You proceed by telling Linda what you have learned about this matter, including specific details, and she eventually admits to telling the two other students to "shave their vaginas." You issue a suspension for her unacceptable behavior, but she would not learn her lesson.

A couple of weeks later, Linda again demonstrates her propensity toward perversion, as she tries three times to grab a male student's genitalia on the school bus. The victim's mother calls you about this ordeal and she wants it handled appropriately.

You begin this investigation by speaking with several other students who take the same bus to get their accounts of what had taken place. You then call Linda into your office to discuss this matter with her.

As with the previous incident, Linda proceeds to lie about this situation. It's not until you tell her what you have learned from eyewitnesses on the bus that she starts to crack.

Eventually, Linda confesses and you issue another harsh suspension. This time, though, you know full well that you will be seeing her again.

True to form, one week later Linda is in your office for stomping on the genitals of one male student and kicking another in the groin. The two boys were wrestling around on the floor at an after-school play rehearsal when Linda went up to one boy and swung her foot up between his legs. Then, as the other boy was lying on his back, she brought her foot down and stomped on his crotch.

You immediately call Linda into your office once you hear about this, and the two of you have a quick conversation about this latest incident. You figure there is no sense in beating around the bush, so you get right to questioning her. After some initial denial, she quickly admits to what she has done and you assign her yet another suspension.

With Linda's behaviors in these situations, she acted out for no apparent reason other than the opportunities presented themselves. The victims were not engaging, antagonizing, or provoking her in any way. Because these behaviors appeared to be of a social, emotional, and sexual nature, the principal has the school psychologist follow up with Linda and her mother. He counsels them and refers them to several outside support agencies that could help them address the issues Linda was having in school.

The gossip you had heard about Abbey in the faculty lounge turned out to be an unreliable predictor of her future behaviors. You wrongly took what you heard there and allowed that nonsense to unfairly influence your initial thoughts about her. What's more, you were also initially fooled by Linda's appearance and her deceptive lies, thinking there was no way this sweet little girl could have committed the depraved acts of which she was accused. In these two instances, you were guilty of judging a book by its cover.

The beginning of the school year is supposed to afford every student a "clean slate," but negative dialogue among the faculty about these students can rob them of their chances for a true fresh start. Educators owe it to all students to give them the opportunities to start anew, without forever identifying them with the poor decisions they may have made in the past.

From these experiences, you learn that the most important thing, in terms of second chances, is to look beyond a student's "cover" and deal with them on what they say and do now, and not the stories and gossip that may follow them from grade to grade.

Chapter Ten

Keep Your Hands to Yourself

Every time you turn on the television, you feel like you see a news story about sexual predators. Accounts ranging from grown men preying on young teenagers via the Internet to educators soliciting sex from students are all over the news. Any civilized person would find these stories disturbing, but as an educator working with middle school students and teachers, you are especially concerned about problems of this nature.

There are also cases every year where students make false reports about inappropriate sexual conduct or advances by teachers. Even when these stories are disproved, the teachers' reputations can be forever tarnished. As a result, teachers have to be more careful than ever before when interacting with students in any manner that could be perceived as unprofessional.

When educators suspect one of their colleagues is possibly getting too close or friendly with a student, most will tread lightly about reporting their concerns if they don't have hard evidence. If they only have their suspicions or hearsay to go on, the damage to that teacher's reputation can be irreparable.

There is one particular teacher in your building, Joe, who teaches mathematics and serves as the middle school track coach. You don't know Joe very well, but you have heard from others that he has a history of getting a little too friendly with students. Your colleagues have told you that he has trouble with boundaries and that he lacks common sense when it comes to dealing with students.

Joe was said to have crossed the line with students, not in malicious ways, but rather in more unprofessional and immature ways. The manner in which he interacted with students came across as though he was more of a friend to them rather than their teacher. And you know that when teachers interact with students primarily as friends, that leaves them exposed to criticism, speculation, and judgment from others, whether fair or not.

As a first-year administrator you did not anticipate the number of delicate situations you would be confronted with, and just a few months into this school year, a sexual harassment case involving Joe comes your way.

Allegedly, Joe had given one of his eighth grade track athletes, Tara, something called a "monkey bite" at practice one afternoon. From what you were told, a "monkey bite" is when you pinch someone else with your thumb and index finger. It was reported to you that Joe gave Tara a "monkey bite" on the inside of her thigh.

Tara went home that evening and told her parents about this over family dinner. When Tara's father heard the story and saw a bruise on her thigh, he called the building principal in a state of rage. When the principal delegated the handling of this issue to you, you expressed your willingness to do so, but on the inside you felt uneasy about the thought of investigating a teacher.

At this point in the school year, you have become accustomed to walking around the building and speaking with teachers when conducting investigations on student behaviors. However, now you are faced with the difficult task of interviewing students in order to investigate a teacher.

Even though you know this is a serious matter that needs to be addressed for the safety of your entire student body, a small part of you feels like you are betraying the teachers you have worked alongside of for the last several years. This is your first allegation pertaining to a teacher's actions and you want to make sure that Joe is not presumed guilty until proven innocent.

During the course of your investigation, you speak with Tara, several of her teammates who were in the area at the time of this alleged incident, and the other track coaches. Through your interviews, you learn that Joe had pinched Tara, but he pinched her on the waist just above the hip, not on her inner thigh as originally reported to you.

This discovery obviously does not make Joe's actions more acceptable because one should never lay a finger on a student. However, it is important for you to get all the facts straight because there is a difference between pinching a female student on the inside of her thigh as opposed to on her waist. There is also no indication from your interviews with the students and the coaches that suggests Joe did or said anything else inappropriate with Tara, or any other students for that matter.

You share the findings of your investigation with the building principal and she follows up with a one on one conversation with Joe. No formal discipline is issued and he is fortunate that a letter on this incident was not placed in his personnel file.

Unfortunately, Joe did not learn to keep his hands to himself.

Two months later, Joe is in the main office during the daily announcements while the Pledge of Allegiance is being recited over the PA system. Everyone in the office—teachers, parents, students, and secretaries—are standing and facing the flag to pledge their allegiance. Joe notices a female student facing the flag with her back to him, wearing a sweatshirt with the hood covering her head. Joe decides to reach forward and pull the hood back off of her head to teach proper respect for the Pledge. After pulling her hood back, Joe sees that this person is bald.

"Which student is this?" Joe must have been thinking to himself. Then she turns around. Joe sees that this is not a student at all. The bald head actually belongs to a student's mother. This parent had come into the main office to bring lunch in for her daughter when the daily announcements happened to begin. She was wearing her hood up as she is a cancer survivor who had just lost all of her hair due to chemo. She is absolutely livid when Joe takes it upon himself to pull her hood from atop her head. She is as angry at Joe as Tara's father was when he heard about the "monkey bite."

It has been a rough couple of months for Joe and you are stunned that he has not learned to keep his hands to himself. Luckily for you, though, you do not have to be involved in this investigation. In fact, there is no investigation needed here because plenty of people were in the main office and witnessed what happened. The building principal handles this one without you.

Following this incident, Joe is assigned a punishment commonly dealt to tenured teachers who get themselves into significant trouble. This time, Joe does receive a letter in his personnel file and the district removes him from his coaching and teaching positions for the remainder of the school year.

Joe is transferred to work in the district's central office, where he spends the remainder of the school year stuffing envelopes in a small closet-like space, far away from students and parents. Joe forgot one of the most important rules we all learn at a very young age. As we are first taught in kindergarten, keep your hands to yourself.

In terms of your handling of the initial issue, you did a nice job to remain impartial and conduct the interviews related to a teacher's actions in a professional and unbiased manner. As a result, you collected the relevant facts of the situation and reported your findings to the principal. Joe was deemed innocent of sexual harassment, but in your opinion, he was clearly guilty of stupidity when he put his hands on a student.

You, yourself, never had an issue with putting your hands on a student, either as a friendly gesture, out of frustration, or for any reason in between. You know it is just a bad idea because as much as you may like a student and want to give them a pat on the back for a job well done, you will leave yourself exposed. If someone else sees this and thinks the worst or if that student goes home and tells his parents that you "touched him," you will regret it for a long time to come. An innocent gesture such as this could bring your character, and career, into question.

In your current position, it is also a good idea to keep your office door open when you are speaking with "certain students." "Certain students" refers to the students you have come to know who are habitual liars or who demonstrate a clear lack of conscience. Whether from information you have collected from colleagues or from your own experiences and interactions with these students, something tells you to be wary of them. You feel strongly that you cannot trust these students in a one on one situation and you would not put it past them to make up some wild accusation about you if they had the chance.

You, therefore, should always make a point to leave your office door ajar when speaking with these "certain students." This way, your secretary or other individuals outside of your office can hear what is being said. If you find yourself in situations where you need to close your door to have confidential conversations with these students, then you should make sure to call another staff member into the room with you. This way, you are not alone and you have another set of eyes and ears to attest to these interactions if need be.

Don't learn the hard way. In a society where anyone can say anything about you that can automatically bring your integrity, as well as your livelihood, into question, you have to protect yourself. You never want to leave yourself vulnerable should someone decide to misinterpret or make up lies about your conduct, and taking these simple measures can safeguard you from such accusations.

Chapter Eleven

You Just Don't Understand

There are some choices middle school students make that you will never understand. For example, why do they choose not to lock up their valuables in school? After repeated reminders to do so from the faculty and staff, students still disregard these warnings and, sure enough, their valuables continue to disappear. Students have their smart phones, tablets, jewelry, and money stolen nearly every day because they fail to heed your warnings and lock their property up in their lockers.

You also don't understand why some students would choose not to report sexual harassment when they are violated by other students. You realize that middle schoolers are at an age when their hormones start influencing their actions, but you cannot understand how incidents of inappropriate touching or unwelcomed sexual advances can go on for an extended period of time without the victim telling someone.

In one example, a female student, Zoe, was supposedly touched and groped inappropriately by a male student, Brandon, in her technology class. However, Zoe never came to you to report this. You actually learn of this situation from a student witness in the same class who chose to come forward and tell you about it.

After speaking with this student witness, you deem this information to be credible and proceed to conduct one on one interviews with other students in that class. From their similar accounts, it becomes clear to you that this did indeed happen and is most definitely a sexual harassment issue. Disappointing but not surprising, when you speak with the teacher of the class he says that he did not witness anything of this nature.

What makes this case unusual is that the only student who is denying that any harassment has taken place, outside of the offender, is Zoe herself. You suspect she is so frightened of what Brandon would do to her if she told that she flat-out denies that any inappropriate touching of a sexual nature has ever occurred. Even after your numerous reassurances to her that your conversation is confidential, Zoe refuses to confirm anything that you found from your investigation. You find yourself wishing that Zoe would be more vocal and stand up for herself, like Sharon did when she was harassed by Nate in their music class.

Because Zoe denies being groped, it makes it impossible for you to issue a consequence and hold Brandon accountable. Even with consistent eyewitness accounts from a number of students in the class, without confirmation from the victim, a confession from the alleged guilty party, or eyewitness accounts from the teacher, you know you do not have anything you can make stick.

You try sending Zoe to her guidance counselor to see if she will open up to her, but to no avail. She continues to deny that anything has happened. While you are perplexed by Zoe's silence, you can't just forget about these allegations. You believe something went on here and even though Zoe is not confirming that any inappropriate touching took place, you have to try to do something.

You look up both Zoe's and Brandon's class schedules and contact the teachers of the classes they have in common. Speaking with those teachers, you ask them to make sure that their seats are separated, that they are not in the same groups during class activities, and to keep an eye on both students and let you know the instant they observe anything inappropriate between them.

For the remainder of the year, you make sure to periodically touch base with Zoe's teachers to check in on her. Fortunately, no similar incidents are reported and given that you could not get her to confide in you and tell you what was really going on, you feel you did the best you could for Zoe given the circumstances of this situation.

Another serious situation you had trouble comprehending involved one honors-level student granting the request of another student to whom you never thought she would have consented. This was a situation where the hormones of one student, and the innocence of another, combined for a terrible outcome.

Matt, a suave eighth grader with long, black hair, carries an exuberant confidence. Perhaps he gained his confidence from his involvement on the school soccer and basketball teams. He is a talented athlete, which makes him quite popular among the other students. Many of his peers look up to him and even seek to emulate him, which is quite concerning to you considering your knowledge of his past behaviors.

The year before your current appointment, Matt made a deal with a female student on the school bus. He told her if she pulled up her shirt, then in return, he would pull down his pants. She fulfilled her end of the deal. He did not. This incident resulted in a suspension for Matt, and the hope was that he would learn a lesson about his inappropriate sexual propositions.

Alas, he did not.

This year Matt does something much worse. He propositions a different female student, Anna, whom you never expected would consider his suggestion.

Anna is a model student who takes honors-level classes, volunteers for community service, and displays true leadership potential. Her innocence and book smarts, though, are no match for Matt, who is able to crack through the good-girl exterior.

Matt was sweet talking Anna one day and told her to send him nude photos of herself. Shockingly, she complied with his request. When Matt received the photos, he sent them to several of his friends. Those friends shared them with their friends, and so on, until pretty much everyone in the building had these photos. Given her squeaky clean record and the good head she had on her shoulders, you are astonished by Anna's decision to comply with this request.

When you learn of this situation, you call Anna's parents to inform them that nude photos of their daughter are going around the school. They are completely baffled and very disappointed as a result of their daughter's poor choices. They did not see this coming either.

When you contact Matt's mother regarding this issue, she becomes very upset with her son's antics as well. Matt's mother does some leg work at her house and locates a file containing the nude photos of Anna. Mom comes to the school with a thumb drive of the naked photos and hands it over to you with a despairing expression. "Some of those pictures," she says, shaking her head, "I just don't know."

The reality is that these photos could be classified as child pornography and you do not want them in your hands for a second longer than they need to be. After receiving the thumb drive from Matt's mother, you immediately go to the principal's office and hand it over to her. Once it is out of your hands, so is the investigation.

You genuinely feel bad for both young girls, Zoe and Anna, and you wonder if there was anything else you could have done to address these situations.

With Zoe, you could have called home and informed her parents. Even though you did not have anything "air tight," given that both Zoe and Brandon denied that anything had happened, a phone call home to inform Zoe's mother and father may have been the prudent thing to do given what you were hearing.

Mom and dad may get angry with you, or they may appreciate your phone call, but either way your call will open up the lines of communication between Zoe and her parents on this issue—and that is the goal here. Then, if Zoe confirms to her parents that something has happened, and they come back and share this information with you, then you can follow up and hold Brandon accountable.

With Anna's situation and the nude photos, unfortunately, there is really nothing additional that you could have done when addressing this issue. Sometimes kids make poor choices and they need to learn from their mistakes. It is sad, but with the Internet and digital media being what it is, those pictures of her will be "out there" forever.

In your building, you see approximately one sexual harassment case per week, and you can only imagine how high that number would be if each and every instance was actually reported. It's hard for you to wrap your head around how so many of these middle school kids, at thirteen or fourteen years of age, can behave so heinously and make such poor choices. You wonder if maybe you are just out of touch.

Now that you are an administrator and dealing with these issues, you can attest that kids are really growing up a lot faster than they used to—and you don't mean "growing up" in a good way.

Chapter Twelve

Let's Get Ready to Rumble

As a school building administrator in this socioeconomically diverse middle school, you have already dealt with over a dozen fights and you are only three months into this school year. In fact, fights have been so common that you are learning to expect them as this year goes on. And these fights were not little scuffles either. These were *real* brawls with *real* punches, resulting in *real* bloody lips, *real* broken noses, and *real* concussions.

You've come to accept the reality that middle school students in your building fight quite often, as it is engrained in the culture of the community in which they grew up.

One time, two small male students got into a fight in the building lobby. A hall monitor broke them apart within thirty seconds, but that was plenty of time for each of them to land a few good punches. One of the boys emerged with several knots bulging from his forehead, and the other had two fat, bloody lips.

You never would have thought these two tiny eighth grade boys could have done such damage to each other no matter how long the fight lasted, but each of their punches landed with significant impact. After speaking with both boys in your office, you learned that they fought because one student allegedly said something about the other student's mother. As silly as the reason for the fight was, it was still a fight and both boys were suspended.

Another fight you will never forget took place after school, and just thinking about what happened to the loser still makes you cringe:

One afternoon shortly before dismissal, you get wind of a showdown scheduled to take place after school between two boys, Aaron and Vince. When you hear these rumors, you do what you can to stop it from happening. Following your normal procedures, you speak with Aaron and Vince during the last period of the day and they both try to convince you that no such fight is planned. Knowing these students, both "frequent flyers" from troubled homes, you decide to scope things out after school anyway.

Right after dismissal you notice an unusually large crowd of students heading away from the building, down the street directly opposite of the school's main entrance. This is a sure sign that a fight is about to take place. You make your mind up to jump in your car and follow the crowd.

You lose sight of the group of students for a minute, and then notice that they turned down an intersecting street. You make the turn and drive a few blocks to catch up, but by the time you arrive on the scene, it is too late. The fight has happened and the mob of students has completely dissipated. There is no sign of Aaron or Vince anywhere.

You continue to circle the nearby streets in search of them when finally you notice Vince crouching on a curb with his head hidden between his knees. A nearby straggling student sees you, runs up to Vince, and tells him to get up and leave because you are in the area. Vince tries to make a quick getaway, but he is far too slow getting up, as he stumbles and staggers trying to get to his feet.

You get out of your car and call Vince by his name. As he turns around and faces you, you wince when you see the damage Aaron has done to his face. Vince is almost unrecognizable. Both of his eyes are swollen shut, his nose is sideways, and he has a huge lump protruding out of the right side of his forehead. He looks like he was just in a serious car accident. Vince's damaged face is difficult to look at, but you know the severity of the situation and feel like you need to take action.

You remember being told during your graduate course work that public school employees should never take a student in his or her vehicle. It's a big no-no for many reasons, not the least of which is if the driver gets into an accident, he *and* the school would be responsible for anything that happens to the student. But in this case, although you know it goes against "Education Rule 101," you feel that you have to get Vince back to school grounds immediately. You can see that he desperately needs medical attention, so you disregard the unwritten rules to ensure Vince gets the care he needs.

You never do find Aaron that afternoon.

Chapter Twelve

After you get Vince back to school grounds, you call his mother and inform her of what has happened. You tell her that she needs to come and pick up her son immediately and you strongly recommend that she take him directly to a hospital. Mom comes to the building to pick up Vince and follows through on your recommendations.

You then turn your attention to the school's response to this issue. After some investigating, you learn that Aaron and Vince scheduled this fight during lunch over a claim that Vince said something about Aaron's sneakers. Yet another ridiculous reason to get into a fight.

You are able to prove that this crap-talking, which incited the fight, began in school earlier that day. Since the verbal part of the disagreement took place in the school cafeteria, there is a clear connection to the building and therefore your building's Code of Conduct applies. Both Aaron and Vince are suspended for this incident, as they were both willing participants in the fight (even though Aaron clearly had the upper hand).

By the way, when you see Aaron the following day in school, he does not even have a scratch on him.

While you did what you felt was the correct move in the moment, by taking Vince back to the school building in your car, you did put yourself in a potentially bad position. However, you can't be faulted for your decision because you did what you did with a student's best interests in mind. In this specific case, it is best to bring another staff member or administrator with you when you decide to follow up on after-school fight rumors. This way, if you have to make the same choice over again, at least you are not alone in your car with a student. Given the frequency of physical altercations that have happened in your building so far this year, you know there's a decent likelihood that there will be another opportunity to get this right.

You have come to accept the norm that students in your school get into fights often and that more times than not, they are over absolutely nonsensical reasons. It's just another piece of the puzzle when you are an administrator in a challenged middle school. *C'est la vie.*

Chapter Thirteen

The Benefits of Being the Bad Cop

When you first switched positions from teacher to administrator, you were a bit worried that you might miss being in the classroom and that you would eventually end up hating your new job. You understood that you may likely go from being a well-liked teacher to an almost universally hated administrator, but that part didn't bother you. The way you saw it, that just came with the territory. Your concern was whether or not you would still love your job.

Fortunately, you quickly discover the positive impact you have in your new position. You have been able to help so many more students than you ever could as a teacher. That makes the position change worthwhile in your mind.

One day a student named Tina comes to you and reports her necklace missing. She suspects a fellow student, Emily, has stolen it, so you proceed to investigate.

You go into the hallway in between periods and see Emily standing next to her locker, talking with some of her friends. You can see that she is wearing a necklace similar, if not identical, to the one Tina had described. You return to your office and have Emily called down a few minutes later.

Emily comes into your office, unsure of why she was called down. You choose to start the conversation by making small talk, asking her how she is doing, how her classes are going, and the like. You then compliment her on her necklace, and ask if you can see it more closely. Emily smiles, thanks you for the compliment, and proceeds to take the necklace off and hand it to you so you can get a closer look. She has no idea that you are investigating Tina's stolen necklace.

When you unassumingly ask Emily where she got the necklace, she tells you it was a birthday gift from her mother. You doubt that story and decide to make a phone call.

With the necklace now in your possession, you ask Emily to remain in your office while you excuse yourself for a moment. You tell her that you will be right back, giving no further explanation, and you leave to call her mother from the phone in the nurse's office. As you suspected, Emily's mother denies her daughter's story about the necklace being her birthday gift.

When you return to your office and share that you just had a phone conversation with her mom, Emily's facial expression turns from a smile to a scowl. She now realizes what you are really doing. Emily responds by changing her story several times, each time remaining adamant that the necklace is rightfully hers.

You continue your due diligence and check out every one of her stories. Not at all surprised, not one version holds up. Even though guilt and anxiety are painted all over her face, she never admits to stealing Tina's necklace. Of course, throughout the entire process you never put the necklace back in Emily's hands either.

When you return the necklace to Tina later that day she is very grateful, smiling from ear to ear, as she is reunited with the gift from her late grandmother.

Emily, on the other hand, is very upset with you. She feels you were dishonest with her and she is angry about the way you got her to hand over the necklace. Emily is issued one day of suspension for having someone else's property and for lying to a building administrator.

Had Emily confessed to stealing the necklace, her punishment would have been far greater, but you had no admission or eye-witness accounts confirming when, where, or how she stole it from Tina. The important thing, though, was that the necklace was returned to its rightful owner.

You realize that maybe you could have approached things differently in terms of getting Tina's necklace back from Emily, but in the moment you were nervous about telling her up front that you believed it belonged to someone else. If you had been honest with Emily from the beginning and she refused to give you the necklace and tried to walk out of your office without permission, then you would have had a bigger mess on your hands.

Not to mention, you would have had no idea how you would have then tried to get Tina's necklace back at that point. That is why you did what you did.

Enforcing the rules and maintaining order in your school has certainly made you some enemies, particularly among the students. But when you see the fruits of your labor, such as Tina's smile when you handed her back her necklace, you don't really care how many enemies you have. Someone has to be the "bad cop," and you are happy to fill that role if you can do some good with it.

Oddly enough, you actually consider it a compliment of sorts when teachers tell you that their students groan when they hear your name. The way you see it, in this school at this time, what you are doing is a necessary part of keeping the building in order. Your school needs someone in the administration that the kids are scared of, someone to keep them honest.

Shortly after the necklace investigation you hear about a student compiling a list of his "most hated" school personnel and posting this list on his social networking page. You are number one on his list. You now know that you are having a real impact in the building. You know you are doing something right.

Your goal, of course, is not to become the most hated person in the building, but rather to change the culture and climate of your school from what it was last year—and you are doing just that.

Chapter Fourteen

The Honeymoon Is Over

You have heard teachers say that when a teacher becomes an administrator, they are crossing over to "the dark side," suggesting they become an adversary rather than an ally. When you first became a building administrator, you were also told by fellow administrators that things would change—colleagues you once considered friends would treat you differently and your social status in the building would no longer be the same.

While you were forewarned about the shift in perception that would occur when you transitioned from teacher to administrator, you did not see it right away. In the beginning, your teacher friends seemed happy for you. The first couple of months on the job were great and the teaching staff appreciated your hard work. Over time, though, teachers stopped seeing you as a friend and colleague and began seeing you as the enemy.

You finally realize the honeymoon period is over when two physical education teachers, both of whom you formerly considered good friends, show you what they now think of you.

It is early January and school is back in session after the holiday break. You have been back to work for three days and after nearly two weeks away, your plate isn't full—it's overflowing. In addition to your daily responsibilities, you have several committee meetings to plan for and a pile of high-priority referrals on your desk that need to be addressed as soon as possible.

After dismissal on this very busy winter day, you go down to the gymnasium to inform your friend Fred, a physical education teacher and basketball coach, that one of his basketball players was involved in a discipline issue earlier that day.

The Honeymoon Is Over

You always try to let the coaches know about their student athletes' behavior issues in school. Since middle school students love sports and desperately want to play on their school teams, you thought that making their coaches aware of their actions in school was a good motivator for them to stay out of trouble.

After quickly informing Fred of the situation involving one of his players, you head back toward your office and the pile of work on your desk. At that moment Drew, another physical education teacher and close friend, comes over to tell you about a student wandering around the hallways earlier that day.

Drew cannot recall the name of the student off the top of his head. He asks you to walk with him down to his office where he has the name written down, but you are so swamped with work, you ask him if you can get the name from him tomorrow morning. He looks at you incredulously and says, "You don't have two minutes?"

"Honestly, Drew, I don't. Can it wait until tomorrow?" you respond.

"Fine," he replies as he walks off in a huff.

You initially feel bad for upsetting him, so you call to him and say, "Drew, I'm sorry about this. I just don't have the time right now. Are we okay?" He continues walking away, and without even turning to look at you, says, "Yeah, fine."

The following morning, you run into Fred as he comes by your office. Immediately, his body language tells you that he is not happy with you. He comes over and hands you eight discipline referrals from himself and Drew, each more nonsensical than the last—tardiness, minor class disruptions, students being unprepared for gym class.

This sudden influx of absurd discipline referrals is clearly retaliation from the previous day. Drew had obviously told Fred about your exchange from yesterday afternoon and his unhappiness with your response. Together, they chose this course of action to teach you a lesson.

You are absolutely furious because this is a clear case of unwarranted revenge. You work so hard every day and their referrals land you with an additional two hours of unnecessary work—valuable time that you could have spent on more serious matters.

After following up on their eight referrals, you seek out Fred and speak with him. You express your utter disappointment that they resorted to this tactic and that they gave you eight senseless referrals for no reason other than they felt that you needed to be put in your place.

Fred just stays quiet as you talk. He does not respond or validate your feelings. You leave the conversation feeling discontented and you can tell he no longer cares what you think.

The way your relationship with Fred and Drew changed so suddenly really bothers you. Prior to becoming an administrator, you used to play pick-up basketball with them and considered them close friends. On the court, you were pretty competitive and would often banter back and forth, but you still maintained a mutual respect for one another when the game was over.

In the end, though, your friendship did not matter one iota once your position changed. Rather than speaking with you about their impressions of how you interacted with Drew that one afternoon, they used passive-aggressive techniques to show you that you were no longer on the same page.

You wonder, "Should I have turned around and accompanied Drew down to his office to get the name of that student?"

Well, you could have, but you were really busy that afternoon. Plus, it was not an emergency issue and since it was the end of the day and all of the students had already gone home, you could not have followed up with this student until the morning anyway. The bottom line is, this was an overreaction on their part and you should not second guess yourself because of how this situation played out.

After this incident you realize things will never be the same for you around the school and you begin noticing that when you walk into a room full of teachers, everyone would suddenly become silent. Over time, you learn to accept that your new position will unfairly earn you a lot of enemies. The honeymoon period is indeed over.

Chapter Fifteen

It's Not My Problem

There is a timeout room in your building where teachers can send students when they are too disruptive to remain in class. Students sent to the timeout room are handed a written discipline referral before they leave the classroom, and they bring these referrals with them to the timeout room. Once there, they hand the referral in to the monitor in charge and sit at a desk for the remainder of the period. At the end of each school day, these discipline referrals are collected and brought to your office. You routinely follow up on these referrals at your earliest convenience, which is usually the following morning. This is the process in place for non-urgent discipline issues.

However, teachers do not always follow this building protocol. It drives you nuts when teachers bring their students directly to your office for minor disruptive behaviors rather than following the normal building procedures described above.

On any given school day, you can be up to your eyeballs with high-priority issues: a fight to handle, a theft to investigate, an angry parent waiting to yell at you, etc. Each of these situations requires a significant amount of time, effort, attention, and tact to handle properly. It seems like the moment you figure out what to do when handling one of these high-priority issues, in walks a teacher with a nonsense issue about a student talking during their class.

They will say something like, "Nicholas is continually calling out in class and I cannot have him disrupting my lesson. I am here to teach, not to babysit. It's not my job to teach these kids manners."

As you look at the teacher blankly, you think to yourself, "Are you friggin' kidding me? A student talking in your class is why you are here?

Get out of here, return to your classroom, and handle your students. These are twelve- and thirteen-year-old kids. You have a master's degree, speak three different languages, and can play three different instruments, yet an adolescent has got you ranting to me about your inability to stop him from talking in your class?"

That's what you want to say, but of course your position requires you to maintain a certain level of professionalism and forbids you from responding this way. Instead, you reply with something less abrasive. "Okay," you say calmly, "I will speak with him." Even as these words escape your mouth, you know it is not the correct response.

In such instances, the student's behavior is not an issue for your office. Rather, it is a classroom management issue that needs to be handled by the teacher. What you should have done was instruct the teacher to call home, speak with the parent and explain the behaviors the student is exhibiting, and ask them to address these behaviors with their child.

But at this point in your first year on the job, you are too green. You are not fully aware that this is a classroom management issue, nor do you have the backbone to tell the teachers that they needed to handle situations such as these on their own. Not to worry, though. In time you will be able to distinguish the differences between discipline and classroom management issues, and you will develop the courage to have conversations about these differences with teachers.

In terms of the timeout room, it is a good idea to remind the teachers of this protocol in the beginning of the school year, perhaps at a building-level meeting. This way, you can review the measures that are in place when teachers *need* to send students out of their classroom for disruptive, non-pressing issues. Doing this will allow you to reference that building meeting later on in the school year when the teachers forget this protocol and send kids to your office for calling out in class.

Unfortunately, this will likely be an ongoing problem because there will always be teachers who just can't understand what it means to manage their own classrooms. Those teachers fail to recognize that handling minor student discipline issues is their own responsibility. Their only response is to pass the buck to you because they feel that such issues are "not their problem."

Chapter Sixteen

Role Models

When you were a teacher, you would frequently overhear some of your colleagues complain about their jobs, talk trash about one another, and blame administration for everything. It seemed like everyone was a target for complaint.

You could not understand what you were hearing. What was there to complain about, really? Teachers have some of the best jobs in the world. Maybe they don't take home the most impressive salaries, but with opportunities for tenure, summers and holiday vacations off, and the ability to get home at a decent hour most afternoons, it's a pretty enviable job. Yet, there are a few teachers who still find plenty of things to whine about.

Now that you are an administrator, you see that the gossip you were exposed to has only grown more twisted and drawn out. Instead of overhearing your colleagues complain about one another in the faculty room and in the teacher-work spaces, they come running to you when they have someone to bitch about. Now teachers routinely come to your office and vent in greater detail about students, parents, administrators, and one another.

You can't stand gossip and you literally have no time for it, but hearing teachers talk trash is not actually what bothers you the most about certain members of your building's faculty.

One of the most important responsibilities educators have is to be role models for the students. Teachers and administrators should hold themselves to a higher standard than perhaps the rest of society. They need to understand the powerful impact the examples they set can have on their students. Unfortunately, the value of that impact is not recognized by all of your colleagues.

One person in particular comes to mind when you think about poor modeling. Jake is a technology teacher at your school who is well liked as a person, but certainly not well respected as a teacher—not by his colleagues or his students. Jake is in his mid-forties but he behaves like a fifteen-year-old, which makes him a playful and fun person to be around, but not a responsible teacher who commands respect in a classroom setting.

Jake went into education because he cares about kids, but he is very immature himself and he never took the time or energy to develop and master his classroom management skills. He spent too much time joking around with the students and letting them do whatever they wanted in his classroom. In an effort to be well liked, he missed the forest for the trees.

During his class periods, Jake would frequently have conversations with his fellow teachers. While the students were inside his classroom, he'd be outside in the hallway, gossiping with his colleagues and telling them dirty jokes. He also allowed his students to talk, chew gum, throw papers, and fool around in his classes on a daily basis. Jake was even known to fart in front of his students. The bottom line was that Jake was a clown and he had no control in his classroom.

When a teacher fails to establish classroom rules and expectations for student behavior, the students will not comply when that teacher suddenly tries to drop the hammer one day in the middle of the school year. If fooling around and horseplay are permitted in the classroom, students are then encouraged to continue engaging in these behaviors because the message has been sent that these behaviors are acceptable in this class. That was the exact situation with Jake's classes.

When Jake did attempt to take control of his classroom, which was not often, he was completely unsuccessful. Every so often when he was irritable and having a bad day, Jake would send a kid to your office for talking in his class.

How can you possibly punish this student for engaging in behaviors Jake has allowed all year long? The answer is you can't. This behavior is more Jake's fault than it is the student's.

Following up, because you know you have to address it since Jake brought this issue to your attention, you speak with the student but do not assign a consequence. Then, when Jake learns that the student did not receive a detention, he comes to you, up in arms, and asks why not. You try explaining to Jake that he has classroom management issues that need to be addressed, and you offer suggestions on how he can improve, but all of that falls on deaf ears. He probably left this conversation and complained about you to the first colleague he found on the way back to his classroom.

You feel strongly that measures of accountability should be in place for teachers who do not conduct themselves in a professional manner. Effective teaching requires much more than writing lesson plans and grading papers. Maintaining and modeling a professional demeanor is one of the most important and fundamental components of being a classroom educator.

Even though you tried to connect with Jake about his classroom management issues and your constructive and honest feedback proved futile, you should still stay the course and try to help him see the error of his ways. Not as much because it affects your workload, but more importantly because it is the students in his classes who are missing out on a quality education. Observing Jake's classes and giving him feedback rooted in evidence or recommending that he observe another teacher who has excellent control of their classes are two strategies you can turn to in order to get Jake to see the light.

Without demonstrating professionalism, there can be no structure. Without structure, there can be no order. And without order, there can be no learning. It's just not possible, and observing what goes on in Jake's classes is the proof.

Chapter Seventeen

Those Who Can't Do, Teach

In your experiences, and contrary to the case with Jake the technology teacher, most teachers who cannot handle their students are the ones whose path to education came from a fallback plan rather than a passion for learning and working with students.

Some of the biggest pot-stirrers and complainers in your building are specialty teachers in subjects such as art, music, and world languages. Some of these individuals pursued teaching because, while they were primarily passionate about their work in art, music, or language, they did not have what it took to go further in those fields. As a result they decided to become a teacher, which afforded them an opportunity to make a living with their artistic or linguistic skills.

They became teachers out of their love for their respective fields, not for their love of working with students. Many of them don't understand kids and since they do not know how to interact and reason with students, they have significant difficulty teaching their lessons. Consequently, they find themselves far more frustrated than they should be.

Their inability to control their students adds stress to their professional and personal lives, and causes them to be unhappy and disgruntled. Unhappy teachers are easy to spot. Their sour facial expressions, defensive postures, and constant complaining give them away pretty quickly.

Just because someone is able to earn their master's degree in education does not automatically make him or her a good fit to work with students. Unfortunately, there are some educators, albeit only a few, who do not have the patience, understanding, or skills to deal with middle school students.

Teaching is a profession that should be chosen out of love—love for students *and* a love for learning. If you don't really care about children and their learning, don't become a teacher. There is a very good chance you'll be unhappy with your career choice, and you will probably make the kids in your classes miserable too.

Chapter Eighteen

The Apple Doesn't Fall Far

During your first year as a new administrator, different students would come and go, transferring into your school one week and out the next. Many students came and went this year, but there was one student who transferred into your building and, along with his mother, left a lasting impression that you will never forget.

This student's name is Kenneth and he is a skinny but good-looking kid from Ohio. The day the staff learn that Kenneth was transferring into your building, two of your colleagues flag you down in the hallway. They ask you if you know him and you respond that you do not. They tell you that they have experience working with him and that he has some very serious issues.

Apparently, Kenneth was in your district a few years ago when he was in elementary school, but then he moved to live with his father in Ohio. The two staff members who informed you about Kenneth and his outbursts had worked in that elementary school several years ago when Kenneth was a student there.

For the first few weeks Kenneth is in the building, you never hear a peep from him. You see him in the hallways in between periods and say, "Hello," and he always looks back at you with a smile. In fact he seems pretty happy whenever you see him. You wonder if maybe he turned things around and got over whatever was troubling him in elementary school.

Then one afternoon right after dismissal, you are heading to the monthly faculty meeting and as you are leaving your office, a guidance counselor comes rushing over to you and informs you that she has a serious situation on her hands. The situation she is referring to is Kenneth.

She tells you that Kenneth is having a meltdown in her office. You ask her what exactly she means by "meltdown" and she explains that he has been crying and cursing, and that she is a little concerned that he may want to hurt himself. Since you have only heard that Kenneth had outbursts in elementary school from a couple of your colleagues and have not actually witnessed them yourself, you are a bit surprised. Still, you walk with the guidance counselor to her office to see if you can help calm him down.

You and the guidance counselor arrive at her office and see Kenneth sitting down quietly in a chair with his hands on his knees. He's not saying anything, but he looks like he has been crying. You think a change of scenery may be a good idea, so you suggest that he come with you to your office so the three of you can talk. Kenneth does not respond verbally, but he stands up, demonstrating that he is listening to you and willing to go to your office.

Once in your office, Kenneth sits down in a chair in front of your desk. He still looks upset, but he is calm. His guidance counselor sits in one of the chairs next to him and you sit behind your desk. You ask Kenneth what is bothering him to start the conversation. He answers, "I guess it is school. I don't really like my classes. My teachers don't like me and they single me out. My social studies teacher yelled at me in front of the entire class the other day and all the other kids started laughing. Now the other kids are talking about me. I really hate this school."

You can see that Kenneth is getting upset as he continues talking, so you try and interject. "Hmm?" you say, "But every time I see you in the hallway you are smiling and—"

Kenneth interrupts, "And the same kids that are talking about me now are the ones who bullied me in elementary school. Do you know they bullied me and I got in trouble for it? I was called into the principal's office." Kenneth is getting more worked up by the second.

You try again to refocus him, "But Kenneth, you are not here now because you are in trouble. We just want to make sure that you're okay." His guidance counselor tries to chime in, "That's right, Kenneth. We care about—"

She is cut off by Kenneth, "I got in trouble. The principal made me write an apology letter to the bullies." He is now speaking much faster and his eyes are watering up. "What type of message does that send? It didn't put an end to the bullying either. They kept bullying me then, and they are bullying me again now! My parents don't help me either. All they care about is themselves. I hate them. I hate them!"

Kenneth is now at an elevated emotional state and you are becoming concerned. Because you feel a lot of negative energy coming from him, you decide to move your seat from behind your desk to the chair next to him, on the opposite side of his guidance counselor.

Kenneth begins to cry. You continue to try reasoning with him to calm him down, but it's not working. Tears are pouring down his face and he starts cursing loudly, repeatedly saying, "F***! F***! F***!"

You say, "Okay. Okay, Kenneth. Just try to breathe. Take a deep breath." But he can't hear a word you are saying. He's working himself up into more of a tizzy with every moment that passes. Nothing you are saying is calming him down.

He starts shrieking loudly. You and the guidance counselor look at each other. Neither of you can get a word in edgewise. Kenneth is crying profusely and sobbing in between his shrieks and expletives. He's out of control. You start thinking about calling an ambulance.

Now you realize this is what the two teachers must have experienced with Kenneth in elementary school. You tell Kenneth in a firm but caring tone, "Kenneth, you really need to calm down and take some deep breaths."

Just then, as he is sitting in between you and his guidance counselor, he suddenly reaches for the desktop organizer on your desk, grabs a pen out of it, secures it with both hands, and thrusts the point toward his chest to stab himself.

With no time to think, you react instinctively. You catch his wrists just before the tip of the pen meets the middle of his chest. With both of his wrists securely in your grasp, you tell him, "No, Kenneth! No!"

After a moment, Kenneth loosens his grip on the pen and drops it.

The guidance counselor puts her hands on Kenneth's forearms and he slowly lowers his hands. You feel the tenseness of his wrists subside, so you let go. Kenneth is now sobbing quietly with his head down and the guidance counselor is consoling him. You pick the pen up from the floor and take it, along with the scissors and all of the other sharp objects from the top of your desk, and put them in your desk drawer, well out of Kenneth's reach.

While Kenneth is now sullen and crying, he no longer appears to be in a highly emotional state or a threat to himself. You pick up your office phone to call his mother because you don't feel the urgent need to call an ambulance at this very moment. As the phone is ringing and you are waiting for mom to pick up, you struggle believing what has just happened.

Kenneth's mom picks up and you introduce yourself and explain everything that just transpired. You tell mom that it is urgent that she come up to the building right now. Mom tells you that she is at work and that she can come up in an hour when she gets off. You re-explain that Kenneth just tried to stab himself in the chest with a pen, and that if she does not come up right now, you are going to have to call an ambulance. Mom says that she will be right there and hangs up the phone.

Mom shows up to your office within five minutes. She shakes your hand without saying a word to you, and sits down next to Kenneth in the chair you were sitting in when you stopped Kenneth from stabbing himself. Mom tries to comfort Kenneth by rubbing his back. You look at Kenneth for his reaction and can see that he does not seem to be enjoying or appreciating the affection.

Mom is not in your office for more than two minutes before Kenneth is worked up all over again. The crying starts and then the cursing follows. He yells at his mother, "Stop f***ing touching me! You're a f***ing idiot!"

Mom responds, "Oh Kenneth! What the f***? Not the same f***ing thing again? It's too much!" Mom's response staggers you.

Kenneth continues lashing out at his mother, telling her how he hates her, what a horrible parent she is, and expressing how much he wants to move back to Ohio to live with his father.

Mom quickly fires back at Kenneth, "You want to live with your father now? Fine! That's f***ing fine! Whatever you want, Kenneth!"

"I knew it!" Kenneth said, "I knew you didn't want me to live with you! F*** you!"

This is all happening so fast. You attempt to redirect the conversation to the reason you called mom to come up to school in the first place, which is to take Kenneth to the hospital to have him evaluated.

Mom and Kenneth ignore your redirection and continue their back-and-forth, yelling and cursing at each other. You and the guidance counselor look at each other again. You know something needs to happen here. This needs to stop.

You stand up, project your voice over theirs, and say, "Excuse me!" They both stop engaging each other and look at you. You continue,

"This is not a productive conversation and it cannot continue. Again, the most important issue here is Kenneth and his safety and well-being. And again, I am strongly recommending that you take him to the emergency room immediately."

Kenneth remains quiet. Mom glares at you.

Instead of following your recommendations and taking Kenneth to the hospital right then and there, mom begins to yell at you. She starts cursing at you and telling you, "This whole f***ing situation is your fault! If you knew how to handle kids, my son would not have reacted this f***ing way!"

Mom is actually exhibiting similar behaviors to what Kenneth just displayed earlier on. "So that is where he gets this from," you think to yourself. "The apple really didn't fall too far from this tree."

After another minute of her shouting at you, mom finally takes Kenneth, who has remained quiet since you spoke up, out of your office and out of the building.

You look out your window and are able to see mom and Kenneth get in her car. You hope that Kenneth's mom takes him to the hospital, but you really have no way of knowing for sure.

Kenneth is back in school the next day, and he looks okay, but he is transferred out of your building the following week. He moves back to Ohio. You really hope mom gets Kenneth the help he needs, because simply transferring him to another school in another state will not really address the problems and issues Kenneth is experiencing.

You stopped Kenneth from stabbing himself and made appropriate recommendations to his mother that you knew were in his best interests. Regardless of mom's reaction to you and your efforts, you responded appropriately given the unexpected and unpredictable situation you found yourself in.

Chapter Nineteen

The Art of Discipline

Every school day brings something new and different, but there was one particular day that brought you two unusual and unexpected issues from completely opposite ends of the discipline spectrum. It was almost the halfway point of the school year—a point when the students' behaviors are expected to worsen, and continue in that direction, until the year ends in June.

These days the State mandates that schools administer tests for practically every subject, in every grade level. The absurd amount of testing the State requires has led to a considerable amount of criticism. Many feel that because we test our kids so much, they have no time to be kids—to be silly and immature.

Your experiences, however, have shown you that kids find plenty of time to be childish in spite of unnecessary tests. One student found the perfect time to demonstrate his lack of maturity: right in the middle of a State-mandated test.

Daniel is a short and skinny eighth grader with big glasses and uncontrollable curly hair. At times he is guilty of acting out in school, which you attribute to his tumultuous home life. Daniel's parents are going through a very messy divorce and he has not spoken with his father in over a year.

Daniel is the type of boy that keeps all of his emotions inside—one of those kids who seems out of touch with the world around him. Many kids channel their anger by cursing or lashing out at others; however, Daniel acts out in other ways. He likes to doodle and his drawings are a pretty good indicator that he will not last long in your school.

In one instance, a teacher noticed drawings of swastikas and other pro-Nazi references in Daniel's notebook and reported this information to you. When you follow up with Daniel about this, you can tell there is a clear disconnect in his mind between right and wrong. Even as you explain the atrocities committed by Hitler, he cannot see how what he is drawing is so offensive to others. You quickly realize he cannot grasp that what he is doing is wrong.

His actions on one particular State testing day reaffirm your realization.

The State test of the day is an ELA (English Language Arts) field test, which will not be graded or factored into the students' quarterly averages. It is simply a field test, where the State randomly selects public schools to administer the test to students so it can collect data to determine if its test questions are appropriate, relevant, and useful.

Before beginning the ELA field test, the English department chairperson reads the instructions for the students taking the test and asks if they have any questions. A few students raise their hands to ask questions, one of which is, "Is this going to be graded?" The English chairperson replies, "No, but do your best." That turns out to be all Daniel needs to hear.

An hour and a half later, after every student has completed the field test, all seems well. That is, until the English teachers go through the exams and find one test that does not have a single answer on it. Instead, it contains obscene and offensive words and drawings related to substance abuse and oral sex. It is Daniel's paper.

Similar to his response when you questioned him about the Nazi drawings, Daniel does not see what the problem is. "If it's not being graded, what's the point of me filling in answers?" he tries to rationalize.

You contact Daniel's mother and while she is upset, she does not seem to be surprised. You can clearly tell she has dealt with Daniel's inappropriate behaviors before. You explain to mom that Daniel's drawings and unseemly language will result in a full day of suspension. Mom does not argue.

The issue with Daniel is not the only "artwork" you will deal with today, however, and this next art-related situation comes from another disciplinary angle all together.

Theresa is a reserved and ultra-quiet seventh grade student. On the same day your school administers the ELA field test, you issue her a detention for being late three times to her first period class.

When a student is late to one of their classes three times, they are assigned a detention. This is your building's policy on lateness and you make sure to enforce it consistently among the entire student population.

When you call home to inform Theresa's mother about the detention, she immediately blows up at you and flat-out refuses to have her daughter serve the detention. This catches you off guard. You were accustomed to getting berated by parents over suspensions, but over one detention?

As you would soon learn, though, it is not the detention Theresa's mother cares about. It's her daughter's daily experiences in school that have her so distraught.

While listening to mom yell at you on the phone, you learn that Theresa goes to the guidance office every day to eat lunch by herself because she has no one to sit with in the cafeteria. In tears, her mother continues to share that her daughter does not have one friend in the building and the two friends she once had have turned on her and are bullying her on the school bus. What's more, mom tells you that Theresa has an auditory processing disability, which makes it very difficult for her to communicate with other students and make new friends. Mom sums up her daughter's situation by telling you that Theresa basically hates coming to school because of all of these terrible experiences.

Ironically, the detention you called Theresa's mother about was due to her lateness to her first period class, but now you know that Theresa was purposefully missing the bus and arriving late to school because her two former friends are on her school bus.

You now understand why Theresa's mother was so adamant and irate when you called her. She is not really upset about the detention, but rather it is her daughter's overall experiences in school that are weighing so heavily on her mind.

Your heart goes out to Theresa and her mother. You may be the "bad cop" now, but you are a softy when it comes to students who are sad because they don't feel that they "fit in" at school. When Theresa's mother shared her feelings and frustrations about her daughter's troubles, you knew that you needed to do whatever you could to help this child. She's too young not to be happy and smiling in school.

In your phone conversation with mom, you also learn that Theresa is interested in art, so you do some thinking on that. You decide to create an Art Club, with the chief and underlying purpose being to give Theresa opportunities to socialize and make new friends.

You reach out to several other students who are friendly and artistically creative to be a part of this new Art Club. They tell you they would love to participate. You then catch up with Theresa and ask her if she would be interested in joining. She cannot say yes quickly enough. Just like that, you had all of the members of the new Art Club in place.

At your first meeting that same afternoon, you collect some supplies from the art classrooms and ask this new club of students to help you decorate your office to give it a warmer and more comfortable feel. (You initially kept your office cold and drab purposefully so students would not find coming to your office to be a pleasurable experience, but Theresa's personal situation trumps any ideas you had about the décor of your office.)

After dismissal, these students come to your office and work together to create posters, paintings, and other artwork with which they decorate your office. Since the club meets after school, you have Theresa "serve her detention" in your office while working with the other students.

It was a win-win-win: 1) Theresa's mother was appeased because this was not really a detention in her eyes. 2) You saved face because you could rationalize that you still supported the building policy on lateness because Theresa did serve her detention, only in a different setting. 3) Most importantly, Theresa made friends through this club. You recall seeing her weeks later in the hallways with her new group of friends. She was happy and smiling—that was the best part!

So, in one day, you had to suspend one student for using artwork in a grossly inappropriate manner and you also seized the opportunity to use another student's artistic skills to change her life for the better. Both situations involved discipline consequences, but now you can see how wide the spectrum of disciplinary action really can be in middle school.

You handled both of these situations correctly and are learning how you can be flexible with your assignment of discipline consequences while also maintaining the integrity of your building's policies and protocols. Nice job here.

Chapter Twenty

Comic Relief

As with any other profession, sometimes educators just need a good laugh to unwind and de-stress. The heavy workload and stresses of the job make them really grateful when a student gives them something to laugh about. You know the value of a good chuckle, too, and appreciate the moments whenever they occur. There was one student, Marvin, whose very presence was pretty much guaranteed to give you some amusement.

Marvin is a short, unassuming kid with a crew cut and thick eyeglasses. While he is likable and always respectful to you, he is a bit quirky and has a tendency to get himself into trouble. Marvin will often get loud and disruptive in class and fight with other students, and inevitably, he finds himself in your office time after time.

Many students who are sent to your office become frightened the moment they are notified that you want to speak with them. They are scared of you, scared of being in your office, and scared of the potential consequences for their actions. But not Marvin. What you find so amusing about him is that even when he is in serious trouble, he will ask you the most random and unrelated questions.

One time Marvin is in your office, sitting in the chair on the other side of your desk, as you inform him that he is being suspended for instigating a fight with another student. Instead of apologizing, crying, or pleading with you, like other students usually do, he points to a can of orange soda on your desk and says, "Okay, I understand about the suspension. But what about that soda? Do you like that flavor?"

Now with other students, you would assume they were just being insolent if they asked you this. With Marvin, though, you know he is asking that question out of genuine curiosity. He accepts the suspension and wants to know about the soda. You just find it so odd that it is comical to you.

Another time, Marvin is sitting in his usual spot, in the chair across from you, for repeatedly arguing with a teacher. As you are speaking with him about disrupting his teacher's lesson, you see him slowly bend his neck to his right. You proceed with your lecture, but notice that he is not looking at, or listening to, you. Instead, he continues bending his neck until his head is completely sideways at a 90 degree angle.

Clueless as to what he is doing, you tilt your head slightly to make eye contact with him. Before you can even ask him if there is something wrong, Marvin notices the confused look on your face and says, "You're being weird."

Who says this to the "bad cop" of the building? Marvin does, that's who. He speaks to you as he would speak to anyone else, and you find that pleasantly refreshing and hysterical.

You later realize that Marvin turned his head because he was trying to read the title off the spine of a book, which you had standing vertically on your desk, but you had no idea what he was doing at the time. Still, these moments of levity provide you with the comic relief you need to take a step back from all of the craziness.

In another situation, you receive an urgent phone call to go to a classroom because a student is stuck in a chair and cannot get out. As you walk briskly to the classroom, you are preparing for a serious situation and wondering if you will need to call an ambulance. You are also wondering what it means to be "stuck in a chair."

After you rush to the classroom, you find out. You see a student on his knees, bending at the waist, with the entire upper half of his body coming through the back of an open folding chair. He is literally stuck at his waist, trapped halfway through the chair.

It immediately becomes clear to you that this student is not nervous, scared, or injured. Actually, to your surprise, he is laughing along with everyone in the class. When you ask him how he got stuck this way, he smiles and says that he reached through the back of the chair to pick up his pencil, and when he got his head and arms all the way through, he could not get back out.

When you try to get him free, he is not budging an inch and you think for a moment that you might need the "jaws of life" to cut the chair in half. After a little maneuvering, though, you are able to free the student and both he and the chair come through this incident unscathed.

Once free, you advise the student that next time he drops his pencil, he should probably just walk around the chair and pick it up. He smiles and agrees.

Another time, two students get into an argument in the cafeteria about whose responsibility it is to throw out a hash brown that had been left on their lunch table. They keep sliding the hash brown back and forth between them, arguing over who should be the one to clean it up. The cafeteria monitors give them several opportunities to throw it out, but since they both continue to refuse, they are sent to your office.

The students sit down on the other side of your desk and you ask them why they were sent here. They explain the situation, deny ownership and responsibility for the hash brown, and blame each other.

"A hash brown? Really? That is what I am dealing with here?" you think to yourself. You decide to have some fun with this one.

You start by asking the students to tell you about the hash brown and describe what it looks like. Both students look confused and do not answer you at first. As you sit there with pen and paper in hand, they realize you are waiting for their responses. They then do their best to describe the hash brown. You studiously take notes.

You next ask each of them to give you a drawing of the hash brown and tell you where they were the last time they last saw it. You give each of them a pad and paper and sit back in your chair, selling your expectation that they each provide you with a sketch. They hesitate again, but then proceed to draw. You remain stoic throughout.

Lastly, you ask them if they would be able to identify this hash brown in a lineup of other hash browns. Both students burst out laughing. You finally smile and the students relax in their chairs.

You speak with them about how silly it is that they were sent to your office for this reason. You advise them that next time one of them should just throw it away and both students agree. As you send them back to the cafeteria, they leave your office giggling.

With all of the high-priority issues you will have to deal with as a building administrator, at times you can forget that your job can be fun. You got into this field because you care about kids and while your career thus far has been chock-full of pressing matters, the moments when you get to laugh and joke around with students remind you of why you went into education in the first place.

Middle school students can be quirky, silly, and fun. You feel lucky that you get to work with these kids because they can always give you a reason to smile, even on the roughest of days.

Chapter Twenty-One

Real Life

With all of the nonsense one encounters when dealing with middle school students, it can be easy to forget that some of these kids have serious real-life issues to deal with at home. Most students are only in school for eight hours a day. The environments they find themselves in for the other sixteen hours may be full of bad experiences, negative influences, or both.

It is important for all educators to remember this because a student's behavior in school is largely influenced by what they are exposed to at home and in their community. These kids may be young teenagers, but all too often they find themselves in serious and dangerous situations.

You have an eighth grade student in your building, Juan, who was held back twice due to his past behavioral and academic indiscretions. Juan is two years older than the rest of the students in his grade, which makes him a sixteen-year-old middle schooler. Having compiled a pretty extensive discipline record again this past school year, Juan is clearly not making the best decisions.

However, despite his mistakes, you do not find Juan to be rotten to the bone. He has some redeeming qualities—he is genuinely polite, friendly, and bright. You like Juan and believe that with the right support, he has the potential to succeed in school.

Juan's chances for success were limited from the start, though, as he was born into a gang—a real, violent, dangerous gang. His father and older brother were gang members, and that basically sealed Juan's fate at birth.

One day, you get word from your school resource officer, a police officer assigned to work with the troubled youth within your school district, that Juan wants to get out of his gang. He wants to go down a different path than his father and older brother have followed. He sees the lives they lead and desires something better for himself. Unfortunately for Juan, there are only two ways to get out of that gang: in a coffin or by entering a police protection program.

When you speak with the school resource officer, he informs you of his plan to relocate Juan, via the police protection program, to South Carolina.

That very evening, when Juan is home alone, there are two male gang members on his property—and they were not his father and brother.

Juan looks out a window after hearing some noise coming from his backyard. He sees two of his former gang associates trying to break into his house through the back door, which is locked. Unsure of what to do, Juan turns on the outside light in his backyard and hides from the window. When Juan peeks back out the window a few moments later, the two gang members are nowhere to be seen. They had left, but they were coming for him. Juan knows it and he is scared to death.

Juan does not show up to school for two months after that, and you are happy because you believe that he is safely relocated in South Carolina for the long term.

You are wrong though and, in the end, Juan comes back to your school. He ultimately chooses his family and the gang-life over a life in South Carolina without them. Juan continues his affiliation with the gang and he continues getting into trouble in school.

Juan's serious real-life issues at home are a classic, albeit sad, example of how a child's experiences outside of school can explain a lot about why they act the way they do in school.

The students' real-life issues, which you have come to be familiar with this year, have really opened your eyes. You realize that not everyone was afforded the same upbringing that you may have had and you find yourself wondering if you should do things differently when dealing with students from troubled backgrounds.

You still need to enforce your building's Code of Conduct and ensure that all students are held accountable for their infractions, but that does not mean that you cannot take proactive steps to work with and support these students.

Fostering positive relationships with troubled students, like Juan, to let them know that you care about them is of the utmost importance. Connecting with these students every day can help them feel like they belong in your building, and it is this feeling of belongingness that is crucial to getting them to succeed in school. If these students feel that they belong in your school, then they are more likely to have a positive attitude about school, regulate their behavior, and work harder academically.

Chapter Twenty-Two

Priorities

In your building you have almost 1,000 seventh and eighth graders to look after, over 100 teachers to support, countless parents to hear out, and dozens of disciplinary issues to handle each day. You literally have no time for anything else, yet at one point in the year you allowed yourself to get sidetracked because of one staff member overstepping his bounds.

Every year the school social worker, Ted, is assigned a group of "at-risk" students whom he is to mentor. These students are classified as at-risk because they have experienced significant academic and behavioral trouble in school. Basically, these students are considered at-risk of eventually dropping out of school.

Ted has been the school's social worker for ten years, and during that time he has become accustomed to getting heavily involved in discipline issues involving his at-risk students. At times he was overly influential in the process.

If one of his kids threatened another student or even a teacher, Ted would get wind of it and do his own investigating. He would then run to the principal and give a version of the events that sugar-coated the behaviors of his student. Even though his job does not require him to be involved in the discipline process, he always appears on the scene when he learns that one of his students is in trouble.

While you are trying to change the culture of the building from the chaos that existed under the previous administrator's watch, Ted's actions in these situations make it nearly impossible for you to establish any form of consistency with respect to enforcing the Code of Conduct. While you do find yourself questioning Ted's methods when he gets involved in discipline issues that arise with his students, even more than that you question the motivation behind his methods.

During the course of the school year, you learn that Ted's paramount concern is how his at-risk kids do in school, but not because he wants what is best for his students. Rather, Ted's chief concern is how his students reflect on him. He is most concerned with his image and because of this, his involvement in discipline matters is never driven by the best of intentions. He is a selfish self-promoter who has his priorities in the wrong order.

When you first catch onto Ted's antics, you try as best you can to keep him out of discipline matters. You quietly handle issues that arise with his kids and get to the principal before Ted can intervene. This works for a little while, but once he catches onto your tactics, he starts to hang around your office more frequently, regularly questioning your secretary about what was going on.

Your biggest problem with this whole situation with Ted is that you let it distract you from doing your job in the best manner you can. One particular instance comes to mind where you were so caught up in trying to keep Ted out of things that you did not go through the normal procedures in dealing with a fight between two students.

Judd is a student who frequently has confrontations with other students in school. He is an eighth grader who has gotten into more fights than any other student so far this year in spite of being physically smaller than most of his peers. Some staff members view Judd as a sociopath who enjoys fighting and violence, but having interacted with him quite a bit, you see him simply as a social misfit who does not have many friends. Judd acts tough to overcompensate for his insecurities, and that frequently results in him getting into skirmishes in school.

Mike, the student Judd fought in this particular instance, is another kid who gets into a lot of trouble in school. Mike is only a seventh grader, but midway through his first year in middle school he has already earned the reputation for being the biggest and baddest kid in the building. Mike is one of Ted's at-risk students.

Mike walks by Judd, who is standing against the wall in the hallway minding his own business. As Mike passes by Judd, he hits him in the stomach with the back of his hand in a half-joking, half-bullying sort of way. Judd does not take kindly to this, so he cocks his right hand back and punches Mike right in the jaw. Mike is stunned. No one has ever stood up to him like that before. A second later, once Mike realizes what has just happened, he goes into attack mode and starts aggressively throwing haymakers at Judd's head. Judd crouches down and backpedals, just barely ducking Mike's punches. A nearby teacher who witnessed what happened runs over to the boys and breaks them apart. Judd is very lucky that the teacher broke it up when he did and that he was able to avoid any major blows from Mike's fists.

Since Mike was involved, you know that Ted will try to intervene for his own benefit. So, instead of getting right to interviewing the students, contacting the parents, and assigning suspensions, you are preoccupied with trying to find out where Ted is. You are determined to keep him out of the process this time. You quietly look around the building, check his office, and ask your secretary where Ted is and the last time she spoke with him, before you even begin addressing the fight.

Ultimately, you are able to handle this situation before Ted can intervene. You speak with both Judd and Mike and the teacher who witnessed the fight, and you connect with the principal before Ted gets wind of what had happened.

When Ted finally learns about Mike being involved in a fight, he still tries to argue that Mike should not get suspended because Judd threw the first punch and Mike never actually hit Judd back—but by then the principal's decision had already been made. Both students are suspended for throwing punches and there is nothing Ted can do about it.

While things were handled in the end and you were able to maintain consistency in terms of student discipline, you still feel like your focus was off in this situation. Rather than being immediately concerned about the students' issues, you were worried about Ted and what he was doing. You had charged Ted with not having his students' best interests in mind, but in this situation you were the one who had your priorities out of order.

It is best not to let yourself get caught up in drama with other staff members when you can avoid it. You can control only what you do, not the actions of any of the other people you work with. Staying focused on your job responsibilities and ignoring the other stuff is the best way to proceed here.

However, if you do find that you are becoming increasingly frustrated because you feel that a colleague is undermining your work, then you should approach them and have a respectful and honest conversation with that person to share your concerns. Doing this effectively will likely allow you to put any issues, and your related frustrations, behind you so you can get back to the top priorities on your list—the students.

Chapter Twenty-Three

A Visit from a Furry Friend

It is an average school day in February—hectic and busy. The temperature outside has dropped to single digits. It is the kind of cold that forces faculty members to run from their cars and into the school to escape the below-freezing temperatures; the kind of cold that penetrates your winter coat, hat, and gloves; the kind of cold that gives you the most unsettling feeling as you enter the building that day.

In the middle of the day, during fifth period, you are at your desk going through a pile of student discipline referrals. You have a lot of work to do, but so far everything seems rather peaceful in the building. That is, until a cafeteria monitor suddenly comes to your door and shouts, "There's a mouse in the cafeteria!"

When it comes to your responsibilities in the building, you always want to make sure that you do a good job and maintain a safe and calm school environment at all times. This mouse situation, however, would prove to be quite unsettling for you.

You immediately make a beeline for the cafeteria, where more than 200 students are having lunch. When you walk in, things are very calm, to your surprise. The mouse must have popped out from the wall for a moment and then popped back in, so only a couple of lunch monitors saw it. You suppose it prefers the warmth of the building to the cold outdoors.

You take the microphone from the head lunch monitor to address the students if necessary, and grab a handful of paper towels in case you need to catch the mouse (because you left your gloves in your office). At that exact moment, the little critter pops back out of the wall, and this time it wants everyone's attention.

Instantly, the 200 students jump up, stand on their tables and chairs, and start screaming at the top of their lungs. The mouse is only an inch and a half long, but its non-threatening size does not prevent the pandemonium. Even the eighth grade boys who are more than six feet tall are on top of the tables, hugging one another, making loud, high-pitched squeals. You know you have to catch the mouse as quickly as possible to restore order. You scan the floor, locate the mouse, and go after it.

With the microphone in one hand and a handful of paper towels in the other, you are trying to catch the elusive rodent while simultaneously projecting your voice into the microphone in an attempt to calm down the students. You are not succeeding at either endeavor. You cannot seem to catch the mouse and the students will not stop screaming.

Every time you try to capture the mouse, it escapes your grasp and crawls to another part of the cafeteria. Every time the mouse escapes your grasp, the students shriek so loud that your voice cannot be heard over the microphone. This is chaos and you have zero control.

You continue scampering around the cafeteria tables, trying to relocate the mouse as the mayhem continues. You are failing miserably—to the pleasure of hundreds of observers, you are sure.

After about ninety seconds of absolute bedlam, you finally catch the tiny critter. At last, you have the mouse secure in your grasp and now that you have it, you refuse to let it escape you again. While you make sure not to crush the little fella, you leave it just enough room in your closed fist so it can breathe.

Once you have picked up the unwelcome visitor, you are able to quiet down the students, get them seated, and restore order in the lunchroom. As you stand there, huffing and puffing and with the mouse in your clutch, you reprimand the students for their behavior and order a silent lunch for the remainder of that period.

Though this entire incident did not even last two minutes, the circumstances of this situation result in several exaggerated versions of what you did to the mouse after you made your exit from the cafeteria. You hear many different variations about what students said you did to it, including that you "squeezed the crap out of it!" and "bit its head off!" Several teachers even approach you, asking how you really killed it.

One teacher who popped out of a nearby classroom had come into the cafeteria to assist when he heard the screams of the students. "You had a vein popping out of your forehead that I thought was going to burst," he tells you afterward. He is not exaggerating.

You were clearly bothered by this entire scene, which is probably why many people in the building believed that you killed the mouse when they heard about this story.

After leaving the cafeteria with the mouse securely in your grasp, you march straight through the hallway and out the nearest exit door of the building. You walk to the end of the school's property, bend down to one knee, and release the furry little guy. It scurries away frightened, but unharmed.

This was the first time as an administrator that you had no control over a situation. You were quite riled up as a result, but breathing in the cold February air as you released the mouse helped you relax and refocus so you could get back to the pile of referrals on your desk. Your furry friend was out of the building and order was restored.

There's no easy way to handle a situation like this. These types of freak occurrences will come about unexpectedly, and when they do your response will need to be swift. Unfortunately, the only way you can become somewhat comfortable in situations such as these is to experience them firsthand. These will likely be messy and unsettling experiences for you, but that is okay because that is how you will learn to handle these unexpected situations calmly the next time.

Chapter Twenty-Four

March Madness

Every year you were a teacher in this building, you would hear stories from your colleagues about students being suspended for bringing drugs into school. When you became an administrator, you just assumed this would also happen under your watch. However, as winter is winding down and spring is approaching during your first year on the job, nothing of the sort had happened yet. You begin to wonder if your assumptions were wrong.

Then, one afternoon in mid-March, a student named Elisa comes into your office with information regarding another student, a friend of hers, who is in possession of marijuana in the building. Elisa says she came to you because she is concerned about her friend and the choices she is making.

While that was likely true, Elisa also probably came to you with this information because she has been treading on thin ice lately. Elisa is a student-athlete and a good kid, but she made a poor decision this past month. She and two other students stole some alcohol wipes from the nurse's office and sniffed them to try to get high. Although they found out the hard way that sniffing alcohol wipes would not give them anything more than a headache, they still tried to get high on school property and they all received a day of suspension for their futile efforts.

Elisa's parents were very disappointed in her as a result of this incident, and they expected her to stay on the straight and narrow from that point on. Elisa was eager to regain her parents' trust and she vowed to make good decisions going forward.

Given her recent history, you are pleased when Elisa comes forward to give you the names of three students, her friend Amber, Brielle, and John, who all had a hand in bringing the drugs to school. Actually, Elisa almost became involved earlier that day when she was asked by Amber to give the marijuana to John because John was in her next period class. Elisa flat-out refused to get involved and insisted that she wanted nothing to do with it. This time she made the right decision.

According to Elisa, Amber brought the weed to school, John took the weed to roll joints for Amber, and Brielle delivered the weed back and forth between the two of them. However, by the time Elisa brings this information to your attention, it is almost time for dismissal. That does not matter, though, because you are not about to let this "drug triangle" leave the building without some answers.

You inform the principal of this situation and together you call Amber, Brielle, and John out of their eighth period Spanish class, their last class of the school day. You bring the three of them into a vacant conference room, explain your concerns about drugs being in the school building, and search all of their belongings. You do not find any marijuana, though.

Sitting around the conference room table following the search, the three students start joking around with one another because they feel that you have nothing on them. They think they will be released at dismissal, which is now only minutes away. Little do they know, however, that you have a clear enough story from Elisa to reasonably suspect that they were each in possession of drugs in the school building at some point today.

They are not aware of it, but you are going to keep them at school as long as you need in order to find out what happened with the marijuana. You do not know if the students threw the marijuana away or if they flushed it down the toilet, but it does not matter. They are not going anywhere.

You are dealing with three of the highest-profile kids, and three of the best liars, in the building. None of them are going to crack unless you have some proof that at least one of them had the marijuana in school today.

After speaking with the three students as a group and making zero progress, the principal and you decide to start checking the garbage cans in the rooms of their classes. That's three students with seven different classes each, which means there are twenty-one garbage cans to check, not including another twelve garbage cans in the bathrooms and the cafeteria. At this point, with no hard evidence and only reasonable suspicion, you are going to check upward of thirty garbage cans and you are not even certain that the marijuana is still in the building.

The principal and you split up to check the classroom garbage cans. The first room you check is Brielle's first period Study Hall classroom. Wearing latex gloves, you pick up the classroom garbage can and begin searching through its contents. It takes less than a minute for you to find the marijuana. Wrapped inside two crumpled pieces of paper, you uncover a plastic bag containing a half-smoked joint.

After reconnecting with the principal to show her what you found, she notices that the two pieces of crumpled paper have Brielle's first and last names on them. Bingo! You found what you needed. You both return to re-question the students, but this time you separate them to three different locations.

Amber is the first student you interview. You purposefully chose to question her first because, as the least corrupt of the three, you know she is the one who is most likely to be open and honest once you show her the marijuana. You know that Brielle and John will continue denying everything unless you can demonstrate that you know exactly what took place.

Amber comes clean the instant you show her the half-smoked joint. She shares the entire sequence of events that led to Brielle throwing the marijuana away in the garbage can of her Study Hall classroom.

Now that you have the complete story, you can move on to interview the other two, but assuming you will get an admission from either one of them is far from a guarantee.

You interview Brielle next, since her name is on both pieces of crumpled paper. Without this bit of evidence, it would have been nearly impossible for you to get a confession from her. She is one tough cookie. When you searched her belongings earlier that afternoon you found a dozen letters, sent from the school to her parents, in her pocketbook. She was hiding mail sent home from the school in order to keep her parents from finding out about the trouble she was getting into.

After some initial opposition and denial, you show Brielle the two crumpled pieces of paper with her name on them and she finally admits to her part in this marijuana situation. Brielle confirms the same version of events Amber had explained to you.

With two down and one to go, you proceed to speak with John, the toughest of the three to crack. As you expect, he adamantly denies his involvement, even though you have the full story and the marijuana in your possession. After a full hour of questioning him, catching him in lies, and then questioning him on those lies, he eventually caves and confesses.

All three students cry as they learn that they will receive the maximum length suspensions that can be issued in a Chicago public school—a ten-day out-of-school suspension and a mandatory Superintendent's Conference Hearing.

It took over four hours for this investigation to play itself out, including notifying the parents and having them pick up their children. Finally, at 8:00 at night, the principal and you are happy to leave the building and head home after a long day's work. As you drive home, you feel a sense of comfort knowing the first drug case under your watch was handled properly and is now behind you.

When handling these types of investigations going forward, it is always best to speak with the students individually right from the onset, and keep them separated for the duration of your investigation. This will enable you to collect each of their stories individually and compare them against one another to find inconsistencies. Then, you can ask each student follow-up questions on these inconsistencies and potentially catch them in a lie.

Usually, when you catch a student in a lie, their stories begin to unravel. You then expose more and more of their lies until you ultimately make it clear to them that you know they are not telling you the truth. Most students start telling you the truth at this point because they tried lying and it clearly did not work for them.

Taking this "divide and conquer" approach is a recommended strategy when conducting investigations with multiple students involved. When working in a challenging middle school with such a high frequency and number of delinquent behaviors, separating students while conducting investigations can be an effective way to address the "madness."

Chapter Twenty-Five

When Push Comes to Shove

It's a school day in late April and you are standing in the cafeteria doorway, speaking with the principal during a lunch period. As you are talking about the issues of the day, you take a step back to lean against the wall behind you. As you step backward, you feel yourself accidentally bump into someone who is trying to pass by. You immediately take a step forward, turn your head, and say, "Oh, I'm sorry," to the female student you just bumped into.

This student, a seventh grader named Melina, reacts by pushing you away with her left forearm. She then proceeds to use both hands to shove you into the hallway outside of the cafeteria.

You are shocked. You cannot believe this just happened, and neither can the principal, who is standing right there and saw the whole thing. Melina isn't more than five feet tall and can't weigh more than 100 pounds, but she moved you like you were on wheels.

You have no idea how to respond. Just about every one of the thousand kids in this school is scared of you and the vast majority of them would never dream of talking back to you, let alone physically push you. You realize that you need to do something to make sure Melina understands the error of her ways, and to send a message to the 150 students who are eating lunch and just witnessed her push you out of the cafeteria.

What Melina has done is one of the most serious violations of the Code of Conduct, but you have no idea what to do in this case because while Melina's reaction was totally uncalled for, she is a great kid and you did bump into her first.

After your initial shock wears off, you call to Melina, who had kept on walking, and say, "Stop right there." She complies. You then direct her to go straight to your office and since the shortest route to your office is back through the cafeteria, you point her in that direction so she has to walk past all of the students having lunch. She complies again.

Although Melina is a good student who clearly went overboard with her reaction, the consequence for pushing or hitting a staff member is a minimum of ten days of out-of-school suspension. "Is that what I have to assign to a student who has no other discipline history but clearly crossed the line here?" you think to yourself. "There has to be another way."

Walking back to your office to speak with her, you realize there will be one of two outcomes here. Either Melina will show true remorse and receive a stern warning, or she will not and receive a lengthy out-of-school suspension. There are no other options.

Now back in your office, you begin by asking Melina to take a seat and you apologize a second time for accidentally bumping into her. You then sternly explain the seriousness of her overreaction and ask her if she knows what the consequences are for pushing a staff member. She sits quietly without answering. It is clear to you that she does not know.

You inform her that any deliberate physical contact with a staff member results in a ten-day out-of-school suspension. Still no response.

Next, you take the suspension forms out of your file cabinet to appear as though you are getting ready to formally issue her a suspension. That's when the waterworks begin.

Melina starts sobbing and apologizing profusely for pushing and shoving you. You slide the box of tissues on your desk in her direction and she grabs a handful. She is clearly upset about what she did and she finds the thought of a major suspension on her record terrifying.

Ultimately, you are confident in her apology because she has demonstrated true remorse and that she clearly understands her reaction was unacceptable and can never happen again.

You and Melina leave off on good terms and you are convinced that she has learned her lesson. You are also pleased that you will not have to issue her a suspension, and you put the blank suspension forms back in your file cabinet.

Your response given the circumstances of this situation was appropriate, but a student putting their hands on staff members is a very serious offense. There is zero tolerance for students touching a staff member and the response 99 percent of the time needs to be a maximum length suspension. If schools do not respond with this level of consequence, then it will be "open season" for students to get physical with staff members. As a school building administrator, you are responsible for the health, safety, and welfare of not only your students but your staff members as well.

Chapter Twenty-Six

Not My Child

So far as a school building administrator you have seen a lot. Students get themselves into all sorts of trouble and you are the one who has to address almost every one of these issues. It can be trying at times, but you have found that perhaps the most frustrating part of your job is dealing with those parents who feel their child can do no wrong.

Your job becomes all the more difficult when you call a parent to inform them that their daughter was sent to your office for cursing at a teacher and they tell you, "That's impossible!" right off the bat. They continue with something like, "I know my Jenny, and she would never use foul language, especially not toward a teacher."

It does not matter to the parent that several students in the class reported this to you, or that Jenny herself admitted to cursing at the teacher, because this type of parent will continue to claim her daughter's innocence no matter what information you have. You hear this same line of denial every time you have to call home about Jenny.

What kind of a message does it send to students when their own parents don't hold them accountable for their actions? Now you know from firsthand experience that those are the kids who get into the most trouble in school. They know their parents will defend them no matter what they do, and consequently they never learn how to behave properly. Instead of teaching their children good moral values such as respect and responsibility, these parents get caught up in trying to be their child's "friend."

Remember that story about Brielle and the marijuana in the school building? Well, at the Superintendent's Conference Hearing her father adamantly denied his daughter's involvement, even though we had her admission on record and the marijuana was found wrapped in two sheets of paper with her first and last name written on them. He even went as far as to ask the superintendent, "How do you know it was marijuana anyway? Did you smoke it?" Parents like this just don't get it.

However, what is even worse for you is dealing with parents like this who also work in your building.

It's one thing to speak with a difficult parent over the phone or in a meeting about their child's behavioral issues. It's another to speak with a difficult parent who is also a co-worker and has children in the building about their son or daughter's indiscretions.

This is awkward for you because you have to see these parents every day, and because you feel a professional and ethical responsibility to be honest with them, they may not like hearing what you have to tell them.

For instance, there is a teacher whose son and daughter both attend your school and both of them have reportedly made some bad decisions that were brought to your attention. This teacher's eighth grade son has pictures of himself flashing gang signs on his social networking page and her seventh grade daughter has been seen smoking pot outside of school on several different occasions. When you approach this teacher with this information, she becomes angry with you and guarantees that her kids would never do such things.

"How can you *guarantee* that?" you think to yourself.

Since these two items were not school-related issues, but rather just information that was reported to you, there is no additional follow-up needed on your part. You told the mother what you heard because you thought she would want to know what was "out there" about her children. She can choose to look into these issues with her kids or she can decide to disregard them entirely.

Unfortunately, mom chooses not to speak with her kids about the information you shared with her. Instead, in the days and weeks that follow, she continues to tell you every time she sees you that her kids are not involved in gangs or drugs.

All you can do is say, "Okay," and walk away knowing that you tried to do the right thing. You know there is no sense in trying to reason with her anyway because parents like her always say, "Not my child!"

Whether they live in the community or work right alongside you, dealing with parents that enable their children will always be part of your job. However, the more experience you have engaging in conversations with these difficult parents, the better you will become at effectively communicating with them.

Chapter Twenty-Seven

Things Are Not Always as They Appear

It is not long after your first issue with students having drugs in the building that a second situation involving the possibility of drugs in school comes to your attention. Only this time you are hearing that this student, Bradley, is trying to sell marijuana to other students in the building.

A classroom aide comes into your office and informs you that she overheard several students talking in class about Bradley asking them if they want to buy weed. The aide, who was inconspicuously eavesdropping to try to hear as much information as possible, also tells you that she heard the kids say that the marijuana looked weird and that they weren't even sure if it was really pot.

You know your first step is to call Bradley down to your office and speak with him. Bradley quickly appears at the door to your office and you invite him in and ask him to sit down. You begin the conversation by explaining that you have been informed that he could have something on him that should not be in the school building. Before you can elaborate on your concerns any further, Bradley stands up and says, "I am not even going to lie to you." He then reaches into his right pants pocket, pulls out a small glassine bag, and hands it to you.

"That was easy," you think to yourself. You look at the contents of the bag and something looks off to you. This marijuana looks brown and shredded. You open the bag and get a whiff of cigarettes. You realize this is tobacco. Bradley has cigarette tobacco in a plastic bag and is trying to pass it off as marijuana.

You point out to Bradley that this is tobacco and not marijuana because you want to see what he says. He acknowledges that he heard other students suggest that it might be tobacco, but admits that he is not entirely sure. You ask Bradley where he got this "marijuana," who told him this was marijuana, and why he was trying to sell it in school.

Bradley tells you that Fergus, another student in the building, approached him, gave him the bag, told him it was marijuana, and told him that if he sold it for $10, he would get to keep $5 for himself.

Fergus is another student in your building whose name has come to your attention once or twice this year. You have heard rumors that he is affiliated with a local gang, but because he's relatively quiet and stays out of trouble in school, there was never an instance where you needed to confirm or deny this rumor.

Still, you know you need to follow up with Fergus now since he allegedly gave a bag of imitation drugs to Bradley. You look up Fergus's schedule, go to his classroom, and ask him to pack up his belongings and come with you to your office. Fergus complies.

Once you are back at your office, you say to Fergus, "I have some concerns that you gave marijuana to another student to sell in school."

Fergus responds, "No."

You follow up, "No, it wasn't marijuana?"

Fergus answers, "Yes."

You reply, "Then what was it?"

"Tobacco," Fergus answers.

"Did you tell the other student it was marijuana and did you tell him to sell it?" you continue.

"Yes," he answers.

As you continue asking questions, Fergus keeps responding with one word answers. He is not being disrespectful or insubordinate, but he's not being overly cooperative either.

You then ask Fergus if he has any other bags of tobacco, or marijuana, on him and he responds, "No." While you are inclined to take his word for it because it does seem that he is being honest with you thus far, you know that you still have to search him as per the building protocol.

You inform Fergus of your need to search him and start by asking him to empty his jean pockets and place the contents on your desk. Fergus takes his wallet, a lighter, his cell phone, and his house keys out of his jean pockets and places them on your desk.

You open his wallet to look through it and, hidden inside a flap behind his school ID card, you find three more glassine bags containing tobacco.

Chapter Twenty-Seven

Now you know Fergus is guilty of distributing and attempting to sell imitation drugs in the school building. Fergus will receive the maximum consequence allowed by the State, which means he will be suspended out of school for ten days and will have to attend a Superintendent's Conference Hearing.

You entertain the thought of wrapping things up with Fergus and this investigation. You think about calling his parents, having them come up to school, and filling out the paperwork for his suspension, because you already know what his consequence will be. However, Fergus did lie to you when he told you that he did not have any other bags on him. Your gut is telling you that you should continue searching all of his belongings, and since this is the standard practice when conducting student searches, you proceed.

You put the phone call to Fergus's parents on hold and continue searching his backpack. You place his backpack on your desk, open it, take out his binder, and start flipping through the pages. Most of the pages in the front of the binder are blank, but as you continue looking through it, you come across a few drawings. You recognize these drawings as they are gang symbols. You turn to the next handful of pages and notice dozens more gang-related pictures and tags. Fergus appears to have a whole section devoted to gangs in this binder. Drawing and having these types of pro-gang images in school is considered promoting gang activity and is another major violation of the Code of Conduct.

Now you know for sure that you need to continue searching all of Fergus's belongings, just in case you find something else. When you see nothing else in his backpack, you turn your search back to Fergus to see if he is concealing anything else on his person. You have him take off his jacket, sweatshirt, and hat so you can search them. You search all of the pockets of his jacket, both inside and outside, and they are all empty. You next check the hood and the pockets of his sweatshirt but find nothing. You move on to search every inch of his hat, including the inside flap just to make sure he does not have anything hidden in there. There is nothing in his hat either.

You then instruct Fergus to take his shoes and socks off. He kicks off his sneakers, leaving them on the floor, and then removes his socks. You ask him to turn his socks inside out and as he does this, you look down at his shoes and see something inside. You pick up his right sneaker to get a closer look. There is a butterfly knife inside his shoe.

You take the knife out of his sneaker and see that it has a black handle and a four inch blade. This is a serious weapon and obviously another major violation of the Code of Conduct. You have no idea how Fergus walked around with this in his shoe, but that does not matter. What matters is that this is Fergus's third major offense today.

You continue your search until you have checked the rest of Fergus's belongings, including his locker. You do not find anything else of concern.

When your investigation is all said and done, Fergus is in possession of the following items in school: 1) imitation drugs with the intent to distribute and sell to students, 2) symbols and drawings that promote gang activity, and 3) a weapon in the form of a butterfly knife with a four inch blade. Although each one of these violations by themselves warrants their own ten-day suspension plus a Superintendent's Conference Hearing, this is the maximum level of consequence allowed by the State, so this is what Fergus received.

You did the right thing by following protocol and searching all of Fergus's belongings, but now you realize that you probably should have searched all of Bradley's belongings as well. Next time, you will be sure to do this. What's more, while you conducted this search by yourself, you should have had another adult in the room with you. When conducting student searches, it is always a good idea to protect yourself from lies and false accusations students may fabricate by having at least one of your colleagues join you.

Lastly, it is also recommended that you confiscate the student's cell phone and hold onto it for the duration of your investigation. Holding onto their phones and temporarily preventing them from contacting their friends or family members is the neatest way to conduct a student search. If more than one student could be involved, or their parents are extremely difficult to work with, holding onto the students' cell phones until your investigation is complete is a simple, but important, step to take.

What started out as a little tobacco in a plastic bag turned out to be the most significant set of major violations committed by one student, at one time, this year. You learn to always follow building protocols on student searches from this situation because you never know what you will uncover. As you saw with the bag of tobacco and in your search of Fergus, things may not always be as they first appear.

Chapter Twenty-Eight

The Final Push

While you now have almost a year of administrative experience under your belt, summer cannot get here quickly enough for you. You look at the district calendar and count that there are fifteen school days left, not including final exam week. Even though the end of the year is right around the corner, it is still only May and you know you still have plenty of work ahead of you. As spring fever has already crept in among the students, this is the time of year when administrators in middle schools really earn their paychecks.

This past month you had a sharp increase in the students' rule-breaking behaviors. Incidents of bullying and fighting, among other behaviors, have been on the rise. Not only have you had an increase in the frequency of these behaviors, but there was also an increase in the severity of these incidents as well.

Just this past week there was an awful fight between two male students, which took place after school on the border of school property. You did not see the fight firsthand, but a few students who witnessed the altercation recorded it on their cell phones.

You become aware of this situation when these spectators show their schoolmates the fight the following day in the cafeteria. You call these students into your office, confiscate their phones, and view the footage of the fight.

This is what you see:

The instigator of the fight is an eighth grade boy with curly, blond hair and he is wearing black, fingerless gloves. He and his three friends ride their dirt bikes up to another boy, a slow and overweight seventh grader who is by himself. They get off their bikes and the eighth grader starts insulting and heckling the younger, slower kid for no apparent reason. His verbal jabs become physical blows, as he starts slapping the seventh grader in the face and head. After getting smacked several times, the seventh grader attempts to grab and hold the bully's arms to put an end to the slapping. The bully then begins throwing punches and the fight starts. While the two students fight, the bully's friends mock and laugh at the seventh grader as they record the entire scene with their cell phones. The bully had the upper hand in the fight and it only ends when he became too tired to continue. He then curses at the seventh grader one last time before he and his friends pick up their bikes and ride away.

This video, which lasts a full three minutes, makes you nauseous. Three minutes is an eternity when you are watching someone getting tormented like this. No student should ever be subjected to such abuse, with no help or safe haven within reach. You find yourself wishing you were there to stop it.

The saddest part of this horrible situation is that the other students just stood there with their cell phones in their hands, making no effort to intervene. Perhaps not surprising but definitely disappointing, they were most concerned with capturing the fight on their smart phones and cheering on the bully.

This fight took place in a gray area where the school's property ends and town property begins. There is a park adjacent to the school, but there is no fence or clear border that indicates where the school campus ends and where the park grounds begin.

You investigate this issue and when finished, you try to make the case that since this fight occurred on school grounds, the instigator of the fight should be suspended. However, the parents of the bully claim that the fight happened off school grounds, and that because this is not a school issue, their child should not be suspended. These parents' decision to ignore their son's reprehensible behavior in this situation disgusts you.

The bully's parents go to your principal to appeal the suspension, but the decision is upheld at the building level. They then take their fight to the district office to appeal to the superintendent. Unfortunately, the superintendent rules in agreement with the parents.

There would be no suspension and there is nothing more the school can do to hold the bully accountable for his actions. Sadly, there is no justice or happy ending to this situation.

This verdict really takes the wind out of your sails, but the reality is that there will be situations that do not turn out how you would have hoped. Hopefully, that is what karma is for.

As you double check the calendar, you groan at the thought of what the next three weeks will bring. You love your job but are feeling tired and worn out. You need a break and part of you just can't wait for this school year to be far behind you.

Chapter Twenty-Nine

Food Fight

The one thing you know that you do not want to have happen during your first year on the job is a food fight. You understand that because it is the end of the school year, there will likely be a few brash students who will try to start one. They might think that because it is the end of the year, they won't get in any trouble for it.

Regardless of the students' thoughts on this, a food fight is a very serious concern of yours because it can create a chaotic and uncontrollable situation. It can also result in a huge mess for the custodial staff to clean up. You don't want to have either of these issues on your hands. For you, the bottom line is that you do not want this type of blemish on your record, so you will take whatever steps necessary to ensure that a food fight does not happen this year.

As the last few weeks of classes approach, you start proactively thinking about how you can prevent a food fight. You identify a handful of students who have been the most frequent flyers to your office, and you make a list of their names. If you had to guess, it would be one of them that would try to start a food fight.

Since they are frequently getting in trouble, it is not hard for you to find reasons to assign them consequences. You decide to assign lunch detentions to all of these students for the remainder of the school. Lunch detention is simply assigning students to alternate locations, outside of the cafeteria, to eat their lunch.

Now with just ten days left to go in this school year, you have assigned all of the "main players" to locations outside of the cafeteria for their lunch periods. You have also increased the level of supervision in the cafeteria by assigning two additional monitors during the lunch periods.

This increase in staff, and the relocation of the most delinquent students, has you feeling confident that you have taken the steps to ensure that a food fight cannot happen.

That is, until the day when one of the lunch monitors comes running into your office and shouts, "There's a food fight in the cafeteria!" You literally jump up from your chair and race to the cafeteria. On your way there you think to yourself, "How could this have happened? This is impossible."

Once you get to the cafeteria and see the chaos, you realize that nothing is impossible.

You see a mob of more than 200 students rushing to get away from the mayhem. They are all trying to get out of the cafeteria via the doors on the other side of the lunch room. This mass exodus of students creates a bottleneck at the doors. Students are pushing and shoving one another in an effort to escape the havoc. Two students in the middle of the crowd suddenly fall to the ground and disappear from your sight. The sea of their peers, which is surrounding them, continues pushing its way out the doors and into the hallway. These two students are now on the ground getting trampled.

You look around and see a couple of students who are still launching food in every direction. You recognize these two students. They are Adrian and Philip. You shout, "Freeze!" at the top of your lungs and then pause for a moment. "Wait a second!" you think to yourself, "They are not even supposed to be here!" You had assigned them lunch detentions for the rest of the school year. They are supposed to be in the main office and the guidance office right now. It immediately registers with you that Adrian and Philip started this whole disaster.

You roar for them to go to your office immediately. You then instruct all of the other students to start returning to their seats and clean up the areas around them. You walk through the cafeteria to check out what's left of the mob of students who just rushed out of here a minute ago. Everyone seems to be fine except for the two students who fell to the ground. They look a little shaken up, as they were kicked and stepped on. They are complaining of some pain, so you have a lunch monitor escort them to the nurse's office to get them checked out. There is now calm and quiet in the cafeteria, as all of the students have returned to their chairs and are starting to pick up the mess around them. But this view does not seem right to you.

You decide to go back to your office to get Adrian and Philip. They started this, so you have them return to the cafeteria and you order them to pick up every bit of food. You then instruct all of the other students to stop cleaning up.

Adrian and Philip ask you for paper towels and brooms, but you deny them these cleaning supplies. They did this purposefully and had no business being in the cafeteria in the first place, so you quickly decide to make them pick up everything with their bare hands. As the more than 200 students are sitting or standing at their chairs, they watch Adrian and Philip mope around the cafeteria and clean up the disaster area they created.

Watching these two troublemakers closely, you make sure they stay on task by pointing out every crumb and pile of slop you can find and directing them to pick it up. You survey the rest of the cafeteria a second time, double checking for any injuries and other signs of damage. Fortunately, there is no permanent damage to any school property or any of the students' belongings. Also, the lunch monitor who escorted the two students to the nurse came back with good news. The two students who were stepped on by the mob only received minor injuries and no ambulance needs to be called.

Once you feel that all of the food on the cafeteria floor, chairs, tables, and walls has been cleaned up as best it could be, you walk Adrian and Philip back to your office to question them. After interviewing them individually and collecting their accounts of what had happened prior to the food fight, you learn that they planned this scheme during their Study Hall class, the period before. Even though you had assigned each of them to alternate locations for their lunch periods, they both blatantly disregarded your directions and went to the cafeteria to carry out their plan.

As you speak with the lunch ladies from the serving line, you also realize that both boys purposefully ordered an overabundance of food for ammunition. What's more, the cafeteria monitors inform you that once Adrian and Philip were in the cafeteria, they waited until the majority of the other students were sitting back at their tables after buying their lunches. Then the two of them, sitting next to each other in the middle of the cafeteria, counted together from five down to one, stood up, and screamed, "Food fight!" They proceeded to grab handfuls of pasta, string beans, meatballs, pizza, and Jell-O off their trays and throw them in all directions around the lunch room.

That is how the melee started. A handful of other unidentified students returned the favor by throwing their food around, but the overwhelming majority of the population rushed to the exit doors to get out of the way.

There is no question that Adrian and Philip were the masterminds behind this operation and you are determined to make sure that they are held accountable for it. Knowing full well that this was one of the most dangerous situations to take place this year, you have no doubt the ten-day out-of-school suspension and the Superintendent's Conference Hearing will be just the beginning of their consequences. You feel that a much longer length of suspension is warranted for these two students and you are going to make sure it happens.

You call both sets of parents and tell them that they need to come up to the school immediately because their sons are in very serious trouble. Both boys' parents come up to your office and you explain everything that led up to the food fight, and how their sons plotted and worked together to carry out their plan. You then inform the parents that they need to take their children home because their suspensions start immediately. Once the parents leave your office, you start filling out the paperwork for the suspensions and begin writing your report for the Superintendent's Conference Hearing.

In your report to the superintendent, which the superintendent takes into consideration when determining if a longer period of suspension is warranted, you outline the sequence of events that led up to, and resulted from, the food fight. You go as far as to include the dimensions of the two cafeteria doors and how Adrian's and Philip's actions caused a mob of students to trample over their classmates when trying to escape the food fight. You describe how approximately 200 students, instantly and all at once, tried to rush out of the eight-foot by six-foot cafeteria doors and how this extremely dangerous situation caused by Adrian and Philip endangered the health, safety, and welfare of everyone in the cafeteria.

You cannot help but take this situation personally, likely because you actually felt like you did everything you could to prevent this from happening. Fortunately, at the Superintendent's Conference Hearing, the superintendent shows no mercy on these two students. He issues a lengthy suspension that lasts for the remainder of this school year and extends through the first ten weeks of the following school year. While you are pleased with this outcome, you still have trouble grasping how this happened.

Then it occurs to you and it seems rather obvious. You should have made a point to be in the cafeteria for every lunch period for the remainder of the school year. If you were in the cafeteria, you would have seen Adrian and Philip enter. You would have redirected them right then and there and they would never have had the opportunity to sit down. This food fight never would have happened had you been there.

As you continue to think about this situation you also realize that you could have given the list of the students to whom you had assigned lunch detentions to one of the lunch monitors. You could charge this lunch monitor with keeping an eye out for the students on this list. As long as you select a monitor that you trust, you can be confident that they will not allow these students into the cafeteria when they have lunch detention. This will be insurance for you when you find yourself unable to be in the cafeteria because you are busy handling a high-priority issue somewhere else in the building.

Unfortunately, you trusted that Adrian and Philip would follow your directives and eat their lunches in the alternate locations you assigned them to. That was your first mistake. Your second mistake was not making sure that you were physically in the cafeteria to keep an eye on things.

This is a painful lesson learned for you, but one you will grow from because you know you will not make these same mistakes again. For the remainder of the school year, you will be in the cafeteria during every single lunch period.

In the cafeteria the following day as you walk around observing the students having lunch, you think to yourself, "Fool me once, shame on you. Fool me twice, shame on me."

Chapter Thirty

Help Who You Can

There are a couple of things you came to understand during your first year as an administrator. The first is that when you're dealing with kids—and any parent can attest to this—your work is never ending. Your "in" pile will always be bigger than your "out" pile. That's just how it is.

The second realization you had is that there are certain students who will never learn from their mistakes, at least not during their middle school years. They may mature later in life, but as for now, they are not capable of reflection or seeing the error of their ways. These students are the repeat offenders—the ones you see in your office over and over for the same types of problems.

Veteran educators have told you, "There are some kids you can help, and there are some kids you can't. Spend your time on the kids you can help." This is the reality some administrators and teachers have come to accept, but you have struggled coming to terms with this notion.

When you first started in this position back in September, you were trying to change the world one student at a time. A student would come to your office after a fight or an obscene verbal exchange with a teacher. You would speak with the student about what led up to the situation and coach them on how to make better choices going forward. Your belief was that through your conversation with them, you had helped them grow and they had truly learned how to avoid making this type of mistake again.

But this student would come back to your office a day or two later for the same exact reason. You would speak with them again about the impact their decisions are having on their lives both in and out of school, and you hoped that this time you had helped them open their eyes.

When they were sent to your office a third and fourth time for similar behaviors, you realized that what you were doing was not working.

You decided to reach out to the school psychologists, guidance counselors, and fellow administrators who have had experience working with these students for help in getting through to these kids. You also contacted the parents of these students to remind them that you and the school are here to support them in any way you can.

Unfortunately, regardless of any of the measures you took—calling home, warnings, parent and student meetings, conferences with colleagues, issuing detentions and suspensions—these particular students continued to exhibit the same behaviors. They were so accustomed to getting into trouble in school that any response to intervention you employed had no effect on them.

The advice and guidance you tried to provide these students in your conversations with them fell on deaf ears. The consequences bared no lessons learned either. All these failed attempts may have taken a toll on the outlook you have on student transformation.

While you never gave up on these students, over time you were no longer surprised when you saw them in your office time and time again for the same reasons. You had to accept that you would not be the one to open their eyes and you knew that the potential impact you had on turning their futures around became less likely with each passing day.

You should do your best not to let the lack of success you experience in trying to get through to the students change your efforts toward making them feel like they "belong" in your building. Rather, think outside the box for different ways you can motivate them. Learning what their interests are and developing strategies to change their views of school that incorporate those interests is a good approach when your initial efforts to get them to make better decisions have proved unsuccessful.

Chapter Thirty-One

School's Out for Summer

It's June 18, the last day of the school year, and you are sitting in your office in disbelief at how quickly this year has passed. It hadn't seemed to go by that fast when you were dealing with all of those aforementioned issues.

You have about an hour left before you can go home, but since most students have finished their final exams already, there's not much more for you to do. Barring any unexpected tragedies, your work for the school year finished earlier today, during the World Language finals. There were a lot of troublemakers taking that particular exam, and you felt like you could not relax until they were out of the building and done for the school year. Now that they have left for the summer, you can sit back and relax during your last hour in the building.

As you breathe a deep sigh of relief for making it through your first year as a school building administrator, you reflect on the events of the past ten months. You flip through the pages of the student yearbook; seeing the faces of these students brings back a lot of memories, some good and some bad.

One thing that occurs to you as you scan the photographs of the "frequent flyers" is that while you did a lot of good things this year, you also made plenty of mistakes.

You recall entering this position and thinking that you were well prepared for this new challenge. As you reflect back on some of the more difficult situations you found yourself in this year, you realize how little you actually knew. Fortunately, you learned a lot over the course of the year and gained some valuable lessons from your experiences.

One of the most important lessons you learned was that you needed to *slow down*.

On a daily basis you would frantically try to address every student issue that came to you in an effort to do the best job you could and finish all of your work each day. But that goal could never be realized because the workload was insurmountable. You learned the hard way that you needed to take your time and pace yourself, because you are never going to get to everything each day.

You recall one day in the middle of the year when you were speaking with a parent regarding his eighth grade son and the school bus. His son, Bill, had been yelling profanities on the school bus, and after previously warning him a couple of times for the same infraction, you suspended him from riding the bus.

You called Bill's father to inform him of why his son was being suspended from the school bus for two weeks.

Bill's father's question was, "How are you going to suspend my son from the bus when you never informed me of this situation? You said you gave him warnings, but I didn't know about them. I never received a phone call, and if I had, then I would have addressed it with my son."

You paused for a minute to reflect and buy some time. You finally responded, "I will call you back, sir."

He was absolutely right. You realized you had never called him about the first two warnings you issued to his son. You were so busy running around trying to take care of everything else on your plate that you missed these important steps of the discipline process.

You had already spoken with Bill, issued the consequence, informed the bus garage, and recorded this incident in the student's file. Since the parent was correct in this situation, that meant the bus suspension could not stand. All of the work you had already done was a waste of time, and wasting time was the one thing you felt you could not afford to do. There was not enough time in the day as it was.

This pushed you over the edge. Although this may sound like a minor issue to others, after running yourself ragged and stressing yourself out beyond your own awareness for five months, this mistake was the final straw.

You hung up the phone, got up from your chair, and headed for the main office. You walked straight into the principal's office, closed the door behind you, sat down on her couch, and started to cry. You had been running so fast for so long that your mind and body had had enough. You did not even say a word and the principal didn't either. She just came over to the couch, sat next to you, and rubbed your back. You continued crying on that couch for a good five minutes.

After trying to regain your composure, you left the principal's office to get back to work, but you were drained. You had no gas left in your tank and it was at that point that you knew you could not continue like this.

Just as you have advised the students that they should learn from their mistakes, you tried to do the same. From this situation, you learned that you needed to slow down for your own health and sanity, and for the sake of handling things the right way the first time around.

Though it was a challenging year, with numerous difficult circumstances, this was one of the most valuable and life-changing years of your career. Even in situations when the outcomes were not what you wanted them to be, you know that all of your hard work made a difference—both in the students' lives and building as a whole.

If you can take one thing away from this book, try to understand where your students come from and do whatever you can to work with them, because kids today really do have all types of stresses and pressures coming from seemingly every angle.

They say that those who "can't do" teach, but let's see those who "can do" try their hand at working in a school. As you now know, a lot more goes on in public schools than outsiders may be aware of.

Okay, well your last hour is up and you can go home. Your first year as a building administrator is in the books. You are looking forward to getting some rest and relaxation over the summer because September will be here before you know it and there will be 500 new middle schoolers—each with their own personalities, backgrounds, and set of past experiences—heading your way.

www.ingramcontent.com/pod-product-compliance
Lightning Source LLC
Chambersburg PA
CBHW020752230426
43665CB00009B/570